The Bestseller Code

The Bestseller Code

JODIE ARCHER AND MATTHEW L. JOCKERS

ALLEN LANE

an imprint of

PENGUIN BOOKS

ALLEN LANE

UK | USA | Canada | Ireland | Australia
India | New Zealand | South Africa

Penguin Books is part of the Penguin Random House group of companies whose
addresses can be found at global.penguinrandomhouse.com

First published in the United States of America by St. Martin's Press 2016
First published in Great Britain by Allen Lane 2016
001

www.greenpenguin.co.uk

MIX
Paper from
responsible sources
FSC
www.fsc.org   FSC® C018179

Penguin Random House is committed to a
sustainable future for our business, our readers
and our planet. This book is made from Forest
Stewardship Council® certified paper.

For Andrew, a father, and Angela, a wife

CONTENTS

ACKNOWLEDGMENTS

We are the types to call someone up and take them for a glass of wine to say thanks, or even stop by their place with a bottle. But writing this book has taught us that there are many unspoken duties of any respectable author, and not fulfilling them is just not a good idea. The formal acknowledgments page is likely one of them. So, to Don Fehr and his support team at Trident Media Group, thank you. Daniela Rapp and the team at St. Martin's Press in New York, thank you. Laura Stickney and the team at Penguin Press in London, thank you. Thanks to Aaron Dominguez and Emelie Harstad at the University of Nebraska. Thanks to Andrea Lunsford, Ramon Saldivar, and Sianne Ngai at Stanford University. Thanks to Gabi Kirilloff, Yeojin Kim, and Mark Bessen. Thanks to Bridget Flynn, Janet Warham, Matthew A. and Audrey Jockers. Rob McDonald, thank you. Stephen and Jenny Whitehead, thank you. Elizabeth Wood and Dan Powers, thank you. Bodi Mack, thank you, too.

You can all claim your glass of wine from us anytime (except for the kids).

THE **BESTSELLER-OMETER,** OR, **HOW TEXT MINING MIGHT CHANGE PUBLISHING**

Back in the spring of 2010, Stieg Larsson's agent was having a good day. On June 13, *The Girl Who Kicked the Hornets' Nest*—third in the series from a previously unknown author—debuted at number one in hardback in the *New York Times*. You can imagine the lists would have been a pleasing sight over morning coffee. *Hornets' Nest* straight in at the top, *Dragon Tattoo* at number one in two paperback formats, and *The Girl Who Played with Fire* a roundly satisfying number two. This had been going on for forty-nine weeks in the U.S., and for three solid years in Europe. It would have been hard not to be smug.

The following month Amazon would announce Larsson was the first author ever to sell a million copies on the Kindle, and over the next two years sales in all editions would top seventy-five million. Not bad for an unknown political activist–turned-novelist from a little Scandinavian country, especially one who had chosen a rather uncharming title in Swedish and had written some brutal scenes of rape and torture. *Men Who Hate Women*—or *The Girl with the Dragon Tattoo* as it was renamed in English—was the sensation book of the year in more than thirty countries.

The press didn't understand the success. Major newspapers commissioned opinion pieces on what on earth was going on in the book world. Why this book? Why the frenzy? What was the secret? Who could have known?

Answers were lackluster. Reviewers scratched their heads about it. They found fault with the novel's structure, style, plotting, and character. They groaned over the translations. They complained about the stupidity of the reading public. But still copies sold as fast as they were printed—whether you were in the UK, the U.S., in Japan, or in Germany; whether you were male, female, old, young, black, white, straight, or gay. Whoever you were, practically anywhere, you knew people who were reading those books.

That doesn't happen very often in the book world. The industry might enjoy a phenomenon breakout like Larsson once a year, if that. E. L. James has been the biggest breakout since, with *Fifty Shades of Grey,* and unlike Larsson she was available for a big publicity tour. Larsson had died before publication. The level of sales his trilogy achieved without even the backing of its author was supposedly just unfathomable. Freakish. Unpredictable.

Let's consider some numbers. A company in Delaware called Bowker is the global leader in bibliographic information and the exclusive provider for unique identification numbers

(ISBN) for books in the U.S. Their annual report states that approximately fifty to fifty-five thousand new works of fiction are published every year. Given the increasing number of self-published ebooks that carry no ISBN, this is a conservative number. In the U.S., about two hundred to two hundred twenty novels make the *New York Times* bestseller lists every year. Even with conservative numbers, that's less than half a percent of works of fiction published. Of that half a percent, even fewer hit the bestseller lists and stay there week after week to become what the industry calls a "double-digit" book. Only handfuls of authors manage those ten or more weeks on the list, and of those maybe just three or four will sell a million copies of a single title in the U.S. in one year. Why those books?

Traditionally, it is believed that there are certain skills a novelist needs to master in order to win readers: a sense of plot, compelling characters, more than basic competence with grammar. Writers with big fan bases have mastered more: an eye for the human condition, the twists and turns of plausibility, that rare but appropriate use of the semicolon. These are good writers, and with time and dedication almost all genuinely good writers will find their audience. But when it comes to the kind of success involved in hundreds of thousands of people reading the same book at the same time—*this* thriller and not *that* thriller, *this* potential Pulitzer and not *that* potential Pulitzer—well, unless Oprah is involved, that signals the presence of a fine stardust that's apparently just too difficult to detect. The sudden and seemingly blessed success of books like the Dragon Tattoo Trilogy, *Fifty Shades of Grey, The*

Help, *Gone Girl*, and *The Da Vinci Code* is considered very lucky, but as random as winning the lottery.

The word "bestseller," by the way, has always been a book world term, and as a word it is relatively young. It first entered the dictionary in the late nineteenth century, about the time of the first list of books ranked by consumer sales. While it should be a neutral term, it has developed some connotations that are likely misleading. The literary magazine *The Bookman* started to print "Sales of Books during the Month" in 1891 in London and in 1895 in New York after the International Copyright Act of 1891 slowed down the distribution of cheap pirated copies of British novels. Until then, no sales statistics had really been possible. From the beginning, the lists— which were printed in each major city and typically reported the top six sellers of the month—were about two things that were new to the book world. The bestseller lists were about sales as the only criterion for inclusion, and a proxy recommendation system for what to read next. These recommendations were based not on the choices of a select few reviewers or publishers, but on the choices of everyday fellow readers. The reader's choice was and still is the only vote. The term "bestseller," then, should carry no intrinsic comment on quality or type of book, and is not a synonym for either "genre" or "popular fiction." While the word has often been used pejoratively by some members of the literary establishment, who have felt that the collective taste of the reading market signals bad literature, the data itself suggests a less subjective and more balanced truth. Bestsellers include Pulitzer Prize winners and Great American Novels as well as books by famous mass-market writers. The list can house Toni Morrison and Margaret Atwood alongside Michael Connelly and Debbie Macomber. This is why the bestseller list is such a rich cultural construct and so dynamic to study.

Obviously there's a lot of value in writing one of those books. There's a lot of value in finding those books as an agent or editor. There's a lot of value for retailers, too—the top few titles alone are why some retailers are able to stay in business and keep selling books at all.

Of course, we are talking for now of value in monetary terms. Imagine a seven- or even eight-figure advance for finally getting onto the page that book you are always telling your friends is inside you. Not many authors command that kind of clout in one territory, but they are certainly around. And you can glamorize the impoverished artist with his pen and notebook as much as you like, but wouldn't it be nice to think of the story you just made up as appearing on bedside tables, beside bathtubs, and on commuter iPads and Kindles in different languages all over the world?

The key sellers of a given year bring the glamor and the drama. They represent the houses in the Hamptons, the fancy cars and diamond tiaras of the literary domain. Hit the lists and stay there for a while and you will be revered, respected, loathed, and condemned. You might be asked to judge a prize or review other books. Maybe your movie rights will be optioned. People will be talking.

Wouldn't it be fun if success weren't so random?

White Swans

The bold claim of this book is that the novels that hit the *New York Times* bestseller lists are not random, and the market is not in fact as unknowable as others suggest. Regardless of genre, bestsellers share an uncanny number of latent features that give us new insights into what we read and why. What's more, algorithms allow us to discover new and even as yet unpublished books with similar hallmarks of bestselling DNA.

There is a commonly repeated "truth" in publishing that success is all about an established name, marketing dollars, or expensive publicity campaigns. Sure, these thing have an impact, but our research challenges the idea it's all about hype in a way that should appeal to those writers who toil over their craft. Five years of study suggests that bestselling is largely dependant upon having just the right words in just the right order, and the most interesting story about the *NYT* list is about nothing more or less than the author's manuscript, black ink on white paper, unadorned.

Using a computer model that can read, recognize, and sift through thousands of features in thousands of books, we discovered that there are fascinating patterns inherent to the books that are most likely to succeed in the market, and they have their own story to tell about readers and reading. In this book we will describe how and why we built such a model and how it discovered that eighty to ninety percent of the time the bestsellers in our research corpus were easy to spot. Eighty percent of *New York Times* bestsellers of the past thirty years were identified by our machines as likely to chart. What's more, every book was treated as if it were a fresh, unseen manuscript and then marked not just with a binary classification of "likely to chart" or "likely not to," but also with a score indicating its likelihood of being a bestseller. These scores are fascinating in their own right, but as we show how they are made we will also share our explanation for why that book on your bedside table is so hard to put down.

Consider some of these percentages. The computer model's certainty about the success of Dan Brown's latest novel, *Inferno*, was 95.7 percent. For Michael Connelly's *The Lincoln Lawyer* it was 99.2 percent. Both were number one in hardback on the *NYT* list, which for a long time has been one of the most prestigious positions to occupy in the book world. These are veteran authors, of course, already established. But the model is unaware of an author's name and reputation and can just as confidently score an unknown writer. The score for *The Friday Night Knitting Club*, the first novel by Kate Jacobs, was 98.9 percent. *The Luckiest Girl Alive*, a very different debut novel by Jessica Knoll, had a bestselling success score of 99.9 percent based purely on the text of the manuscript. Both Jacobs and Knoll stayed on the list for many weeks. *The Martian* (before Matt Damon's interest in playing the protagonist) got 93.4 percent. There are examples from all genres: *The First Phone Call from Heaven*, a spiritual tale by Mitch Albom, 99.2 percent; *The Art of Fielding*, a literary debut by Chad Harbach, 93.3 percent; and *Bared to You*, an erotic romance by Sylvia Day, 91.2 percent.

These figures, which provide a measure of bestselling

potential, have made some people excited, others angry, and more than a few suspicious. In some ways that is fair enough: the scores are disruptive, mind-bending. To some industry veterans, they are absurd. But they also could just change publishing, and they will most certainly change the way that you think about what's inside the next bestseller you read.

We should make it clear that none of the books we reference were acquired based on our model's figures, and figures, beyond the ones you'll read about here, have never been formally shared with any agent or publishing house. We should also be clear that these figures are specific to the closed world of our research corpus, a corpus we designed to look like what you'd see if you walked into a Barnes & Noble with a wide selection to choose from. Agents and editors do a good job of putting books in front of consumers—it's not as though we are short of things to read. And some individuals in publishing have a particular reputation for the Midas touch. But remember that the bestseller rate in the industry as it stands is less than one-half of one percent. That's a lot of gambling before a big win. Note, too, that year after year, the lists comprise the names of the same long-standing mega-authors. Stephen King is sixty-eight. James Patterson is sixty-eight. Danielle Steel is sixty-eight. As much as fans are still thrilled by another new novel from one of these veteran writers, it is telling that the publishing world has not discovered the next generation of authors who will similarly enjoy thirty to forty years of constant bestselling. Nor did the industry find, despite the thousands of manuscripts both rejected and published annually, a runaway bestseller for 2014 (*Dragon Tattoo*,

Fifty Shades, and *Gone Girl* had been the standout hits of previous years), and neither did it publish a manuscript to impress
the Pulitzer Prize committee in 2012. Why?

Well, it is a universal wisdom that bestsellers are freaks.
They are the happy outliers. The anomalies of the market. Black
swans. If that is the truth, then once you find a bestselling
writer, why put your money anywhere else? Why put your millions on a new twenty-year-old writer instead of Stephen King?
How could you possibly know if a new literary author is worth
the sort of investment worthy of a future big-prize winner?

Book publishing is, aptly, full of the language of gambling.
Acquisitions meetings often revolve around passionate arguments
about choosing whether or not to "back a debut author." The
excitement of a bidding war across different publishing houses
might have you go "all in" and spend almost your entire season's budget on one book. The process is fun, and guesses are
certainly educated, but it's a casino. Before finding a home at
Bloomsbury, J. K. Rowling's *Harry Potter* was turned down by
twelve publishers, and Rowling was told "not to quit her day
job." The *Harry Potter* brand is now worth an estimated $15
billion. John Grisham was rejected by at least sixteen different
publishers. Since then, Grisham has written the biggest seller of
the year more than a dozen times.* James Patterson was repeatedly rejected as he tried to get published. In 2010, he sold more
than 3.5 million copies of his three titles that year. Kathryn
Stockett was turned down by sixty agents before she found

---

* The book industry magazine *Publishers Weekly* publishes a list of the top books
of the year by sales.

someone willing to represent *The Help*. That novel went on to spend one hundred weeks on the *NYT* bestseller list. There are, no doubt, many similar writers whose work currently sits discarded on the so-called slush piles of new manuscripts in offices all over New York and London.

Anyone connected even tangentially to the world of readers and writers knows a friend of a friend who got up for months at 4 A.M. to write her novel before work, who felt inspired by a killer story, who knew the muses were around, and who, having sent manuscripts all over Manhattan, gleeful and expectant, received nothing more than standard rejection slips.

Those friends of friends might be in good company. One editor who read the manuscript of *The Spy Who Came in from the Cold* told John le Carré that he had no future as a writer. William Golding's *Lord of the Flies* was rejected twenty-one times. After writing the now iconic *On the Road,* Jack Kerouac received a letter from an agent stating, "I don't dig this one at all." Ursula Le Guin was rejected on grounds of being "unreadable." That unreadable novel went on to win two major awards. Even George Orwell's novella *Animal Farm* was deemed unpublishable, and that by none other than T. S. Eliot. The great poet thought one of the most canonized political allegories of all time was "not convincing."

To publish or not to publish is a tough question. Big success prediction in the realms of storytelling can involve trying to estimate the sensibilities and inner selves of hundreds of thousands of different people. It is no easy job, and often the rationale behind decisions seems perfectly understandable. The U.S. editors who rejected *The Girl with the Dragon Tattoo,* for instance (and we have asked some of them), thought that American readers would be bored by all the Swedish politics in the novel. They thought Lisbeth Salander was a bit moody and aggressive for a female lead. They believed the mainstream would respond badly to a book with horrific scenes of anal rape and the avenging Lisbeth with her tattooing needles. That seems a quite reasonable reaction.

It's no surprise, then, that editors, when perfectly honest, sometimes claim that big success prediction ranges somewhere between a wet finger held up into the air, and the mysterious crystal ball that the highest paid agents and publishers seem to conceal under their desks. Unless the author is already a big name, a James Patterson or a Nora Roberts, it's a crapshoot. Sometimes, circumstances help—now and again your author is a Hollywood diva and her subject is her sex life—but even when it seems like a sure bet, we have seen some of the vast print runs that follow big advances end up in the pulping machine. The public is fickle.

Naturally, every book agent and publisher does what he or she can to understand commercial books, whether that's on the mass-market scale of a veteran franchise author like Patricia Cornwell, or the less hyperbolic but nonetheless satisfying numbers involved with the most popular literary writers. There is a famous anecdote about a now ex-CEO of one of the major New York publishing houses who, when asked to predict a title for a definite megahit, replied *"Lincoln's Doctor's Dog."* The combination of a beloved president, our obsession and paranoia concerning health, and America's favorite pet could never fail.

It was a wry comment, of course, but it turns out that not

one but two books were subsequently published with exactly that title. Both were flops. The literary professor and author John Sutherland, who has written two studies of bestselling books, concluded one by saying, "As a rule of thumb what defines the bestseller is bestselling. Nothing else." He added more definitively that "to look for significant patterns, trends, or symmetries [in hit books] is, if not pointless, baffling." And his judgment seemed prudent, fair, and final. That is until machines started reading and discovering the secret sauce of hitting the *NYT* list.

For the Love of Books

Let's go back to those oft-rejected but now well-known writers. Our model's prediction on J. K. Rowling was 95 percent. On John Grisham it was 94 percent. On Patterson it was 99.9 percent. History has been a satisfying precision check. The model was, however, wrong about Kathryn Stockett's novel *The Help*. *The Help* was one of the roughly 15 percent of books that confounded our machine. The machine only gave Stockett's novel a fifty-fifty likelihood of being a bestseller. Upcoming chapters will get into the intrigue and complexities of the machine imitating editor. Let it suffice here to say that the model looks deeply, and it told us in the case of Stockett's book that style on the whole was good for an American readership, that the themes were generally good, but that the use of emotional language and verbs specifically was not consistent with novels that most reliably hit the lists. This is the book that, when it was published, drew much reviewing attention because its white author had written so much of the prose in the imitated dialect of black characters. Opinions were divided about the efficacy of that narratorial choice: the model agreed entirely with the opinions of critics from the *New York Times* to Goodreads.

So why develop a computer model, you might ask, to do the work good editors are already doing? Perhaps Rowling would have been published sooner with the model's help. Perhaps Grisham would have won a much higher first advance for *A Time to Kill*. But ultimately, these authors found their fame. Editors were unsure about *The Help*; so was the model. What's the gain?

Well, our desire to work on discovering the elements of success is about more than mercenary advantage. Yes, it is surely intriguing that a computer model picked J. K. Rowling, or Liane Moriarty (99.6 percent), or Jonathan Franzen (98.5 percent). Public conversation about human and machine crossover does, we think, matter, especially as far as creativity is concerned. But working on finding viable new manuscripts in a threatened industry is also, if we may, about keeping that industry not just running but diverse. Our work is, of course, about an interest in identifying and explaining latent patterns in our culture. But in more practical terms, we are interested in the potential to launch new authors, about encouraging publishers to use more of their Patterson/King/Steel budget on the young writers who may one day replace them. We care about giving writers of all levels of experience more information and assistance with their craft. We care about bringing people who don't have the right contacts in New York to a readership. Given that the model does not care if you have published before, if you have an MFA, if you are male or female, Hispanic or Asian, if you are beautiful and twenty-five or less so and seventy, then our work is also about widening access, potentially, to the career of writing. Perhaps one day your friend of a friend gets an 80 percent score that earns him an advance, and he can finally quit his job and stop waking to write at 4 A.M.

Writing about books that feature on the most public and revered of lists—the *New York Times* weekly bestseller list—is also an unashamed cry to readers, be they scholars or hobbyists, to join a thoughtful conversation about novels that masses of people read.* Bestsellers are a class of books that are more often dismissed as objects for amusement than studied as works of literary art, or, at the very least, as works of considerable craftsmanship. Yet too much is missed about contemporary culture and the history of reading if we ignore them. Beyond value in terms of millions of dollars, the value of those writers on the bestseller lists is that these books make us *read*. They make us imagine, feel, discuss, think, and empathize. They let us fantasize, spy, escape. The *New York Times* novelists form the core of literary discussion and debate around the country, in bars, on the train, and at the dinner table. We look to them to see where culture is going. We look to them for understanding of our world. We look to them to help develop our tastes

---

* While different national bestseller lists vary slightly, we refer exclusively to the *NYT* list, since it remains the cultural standard and the most important one to the industry. It is easy to find online complaints about how all bestseller lists are compiled, because none covers every sale from every outlet. The *NYT* covers about 75 percent of book outlets and uses data from Nielsen BookScan.

and opinions and to practice our expression of them. If we can bring readers some new insight into their beloved pastime, then we will only be pleased.

Perhaps by now you can tell you're in the hands of two writers who are passionate enough about the importance of books and reading that they have spent a combined fifty years studying and teaching narrative, and another several years buying and selling books for the biggest players in the industry. We have coached and defended the right to love and hate different novels, or even the same one. We have pitched for publication of stories in many genres. We have, sometimes covertly, helped our best students and our wannabe author friends write letters to their parents, spouses, and future editors to explain why they *just had to* give up the sensible life, forget the medical degree, and follow that hallucinatory, ecstatic, and sometimes depressive drug that is a life with stories and words. We have, it is safe to say, totally "bought in" to the emancipatory and educational power of reading and writing fiction. First and foremost we are readers and then writers. Given this devotion to books, it is natural to wonder what in the world made us turn to computers?

Two Backgrounds

There is probably no one more surprised by "the bestsellerometer," as our model has been dubbed, than the two of us. To be honest, the research began with little more than a gut-level urge. It took four years of daily collaboration, and it brought results that neither of us expected despite two different backgrounds—Jodie's in publishing and contemporary fiction and Matt's in literature and the burgeoning academic field known as the digital humanities.

It all began when Jodie left her role as an acquisitions editor for Penguin Books to pursue a PhD in English at Stanford. Her time in publishing had left her with a lingering question, never adequately answered. What makes novels best-sell? The latent, associated questions, were equally interesting: What makes readers read? What is reading fiction in contemporary culture *for*?

During her early training at Penguin, Jodie had worked on the sales team. Sometimes over lunch, she would walk to the nearest big book retailer to make sure that the marketing budget spent on store positioning was being honored. It is common—and this is no industry secret—for publishers to pay an agreed figure for their top books to appear in conspicuous places in the store. Some retailers will accept money for positioning a book on the first row of the first table, for example, or for having a book's full front cover face you on the shelf. These strategic placements are said to help sales. At the time, *The Da Vinci Code* was enjoying its seemingly endless run on the bestseller charts. Week after week, every lunchtime visit would confirm with a huge blue "number one" sign that Dan Brown's novel was eating the world.

After months of this, what became obvious was that however much publishers were spending on positioning books or marketing of "Dan Brown copycats," *The Da Vinci Code* was in a league of its own. Its phenomenal success was about something beyond the reach of sales and marketing. No marketing spend can explain that long-lasting impact on global imagination, not to mention the eighty million copies sold. Such success couldn't all be hype. There had to be something beyond the marketing, something about those particular words on those particular pages.

Admittedly, it would be foolish to claim that marketing and publicity has no effect on sales. Of course it does. There must be some correlation between the fact that the five biggest publishing companies own approximately 80 percent of bestsellers: their marketing budget can, of course, go further. But it would also be foolhardy to claim that the effect of marketing dollars in the book world is at all consistent—there are too many examples of huge spends that lead nowhere, or of self-published, word-of-mouth runaway successes. *Fifty Shades of Grey* was first published only as an ebook and print-on-demand paperback by a house with no marketing dollars at all. William P. Young's *The Shack*, first published on credit-card loans with only the marketing of a $300 website, has now sold over ten million copies. Other very different bestsellers that have risen to success and critical acclaim through nontraditional channels are Mark Z. Danielewski's experimental online novel *House of Leaves* and Chris Ware's originally self-published *Jimmy Corrigan: The Smartest Kid on Earth*, which is one of the most celebrated in a recent surge of graphic novels. There are many such examples, enough, in fact, to indicate that "marketing" is at best a safe guess and not a real answer to the question of why some novels are read by millions of people and others barely sell a handful.

When Jodie took her research question to Matt, who at the

time was a lecturer at Stanford and cofounder of the Stanford Literary Lab, a better answer began to emerge. In 2008, Matt had just completed his part in a controversial computational study of authorial style in the scriptural text of the *Book of Mormon*. The computer's analysis of writing style in the book suggested that theories of multiple authorship were probably true, and the study presented evidence that supported one particular theory about the book's origins, a theory that has been rejected by the church as spurious. The results of the analysis were ultimately inconclusive, but the response to the article, including an interesting rebuttal from a team of Mormon scholars at Brigham Young University, showed how revolutionary computational analysis of text can be.

This work on authorship attribution and "stylometrics" convinced Matt that computers can help us see things in text that we would otherwise skip over. With more research, he found that a computer program could correctly guess, 82 percent of the time, whether an author was male or female just by having it examine uses of simple words like "the" and "of." Matt was not the first to discover that male and female authors have different habits of style, but his work had focused specifically on the nineteenth-century novel. He then found that using just the single word "the" his machine could identify, with a reasonable degree of certainty, whether one of these same authors was an American writer or one from England.

Jodie's reaction to that was more or less "so what?" It was an impressive idea to think that a computer knew a Brit from a Yank, but this was an artificial problem that didn't need to be solved in the first place. She wanted to see the machines solve a real literary problem before she was convinced. Matt had a similarly underwhelmed response to Jodie's passion for contemporary bestsellers. He thought they were fun to read and then forget about. He wanted to be convinced that they contained gold that was worth mining.

That was several years ago. Since then, we've teamed up to explore the hypothesis that bestsellers have a distinct set of subtle signals, a latent bestseller code. Instead of trying to guess what book might sell, our idea was to begin by trusting what the readers had already, perhaps unconsciously, figured out. The bestseller list, while ostensibly a jumble of very different books, represents a weekly list of favorite signals, curated according to the collective vote. Could it be that that collective vote had something to teach? Could our machines detect a signal in the noise? Did these attention-grabbing novels, be they so-called highbrow university curriculum novels or page-turning beach reads, have telling things in common?

If the answer was yes, then we might learn something about how success works. We might even prove a long-held industry theory wrong and make bestselling predictable.

And so we began teaching our computer how to read.

Machines Reading

Computers, of course, cannot really read, at least not in the sense that you are reading this page. But computers can read books in the sense that computers do most everything; they "read" (that is, they accept input) and then parse the input into units that we human beings think have meaning: things such as letters, commas, words, sentences, chapters, and so on. There is a certain mimicry of human reading there, and the more sophisticated the training the more sophisticated the mimicry. The difference between the human reader and the machine reader is that the human understands that the content being read has meaning. Ironically, though, the kind of reading that computers can do gets us closer to the details of a novel than even some of the most practiced literary critics. That's because computers are experts in pattern recognition, and computers can study patterns at a scale and level of granularity that no human could ever manage.

Consider the question that started our research. Can bestsellers be predicted? To be able to predict things, you must be able to detect repeated patterns. Unless you are a fortune-teller, then prediction is all about established patterns. Typically, finding meaningful patterns in words is the job of a literary critic or scholar. Joseph Campbell, the great mythographer, spent a lifetime reading stories written by people all around the globe, and he specifically trained his eye to identify the similarities in these stories. He was a master of pattern recognition. But even with his level of commitment, there's a limit to the number of stories and books that any one reader can examine, and, at the same time, there is a limit on how closely a reader can examine any single book. So there are matters of scale in both directions: one eye must be in the microscope and the other in the macroscope.

Christopher Booker is another scholar whose tenacity we admire. Booker spent thirty years reading hundreds of books in order to put forward his theory that all works of literature, and in fact all stories, fall into seven basic plot types. Perhaps he read a thousand books in forty years. Perhaps he was able to retain more of their content than most of us ever could. But a cluster of computers, once trained, can read thousands of novels over thousands of points of data in about a day, and they have an uncanny ability to reveal things that we human beings either take for granted or totally ignore.

Here's one example. As readers, especially as trained close readers, we might be very consciously aware of the adjectives that a particular writer is using, but we'd probably not be aware of the noun-to-adjective ratio, that is, how frequently the author uses an adjective to modify a noun. That's precisely the kind of thing that a computer can notice very easily, and it matters because it tells us something about description and style. The computer can also scrutinize and compare the ratio found in one book to the ratio observed in thousands of other books. If the machine discovers that the ratio is a bit higher or lower in bestsellers, then that feature has some significance.

Here is an experiment to try when picking your next book to read. Instead of taking a friend's recommendation or picking up a book by an author or in a genre you already know, try reading one entire week's *NYT* list in succession. Do it with your book club or your English class. If you read with good attention, you'll become a bit like our machines and start seeing unexpected patterns between literary and mass-market authors, between books "for men" and books "for women," between the Pattersons and the Pulitzers and so on. Some patterns will surprise you. You'll wonder, for example, why heroines are so often twenty-eight years old. Does it matter? You'll ask yourself if these authors truly *consciously* keep putting their first love scenes exactly at page 200 if it's a 400-page novel or at page 110 if it's 220 pages. If they do, *why*? You'll argue with your friends about whether endings without satisfying closure can or should make or break an otherwise very pleasing novel. You might even want to make the claim that bestsellers in all categories have so many latent things in common that they are practically a specialized genre in themselves.

What's interesting is how deeply readers respond to these things without really thinking about it. Scholars who specialize in an emerging field of "literary neuroscience" have been using MRI scans to map the brain while people read. This research is all about noticing what people notice. While this cognitive psychology angle on how readers read comes from a very different perspective than ours, both approaches recognize that all literary response is precisely about which words go in which order in which sentences. And whatever that combination triggers.

So, using computer reading techniques isn't antitraditional or counter to our usual literary critical methods. In fact, these methods of zooming in on features for extraction and analysis are very much in the service of traditional approaches, and they provide the possibility of gaining insights that were, quite simply, impossible before.

The precise ways that computers can be taught to read and extract information from text are manifold.* The programs, algorithms, and codes we wrote for this study were designed to process books and extract detailed information about each

---

* Our postscript offers a basic overview of method.

book's unique style, as well as its themes, its emotional highs and lows, its characters, and its settings, along with all sorts of seemingly mundane linguistic data that does not easily translate into concepts such as style and plot. Getting at the larger elements of fiction that are typically discussed in writing classes and books on how to write novels (theme, plot, style, and so on), involves using hundreds of points of data. To grapple with style, for example, we measured hundreds of variables: how many times an author uses words like "a," "the," "in," "she"; how often an author uses period points and exclamation marks; how many adverbs a writer employs and the precise nature of those adverbs. These little details tell a reader a lot. Consider the importance of pronouns to the effect of Charlotte Brontë's very famous line from *Jane Eyre*: "Reader, I married him." The computer notices this "him," and how often we hear about *him,* and how close *he* is in linguistic proximity to the all-important narratorial "I." It notices when "I" and "him" appear almost side by side in more and more sentences, with less and less description in between. Of course, that is just what the reader is watching too. Isn't the entire point of so many stories to get that "I" and that "him" closely aligned, separated only by an all-important verb like "married"? So often, this is entirely why we keep turning the pages.

Question marks and exclamation marks are very telling too. You might remember being in high school and being told to keep exclamation marks to a minimum. If every sentence screams with excitement (Oh my God!), and every exchange is a command (Freeze!), or a yelp (Ah!), or the discovery of some spooky thing that goes bump in the night (Thump!), then you risk giving your reader a cardiac arrest. Many exclamation points tell us something both about likely content and level of melodrama, and the proficiency of our author with her pen. Similarly, question marks often indicate use of dialogue, and endless pages of description without it can slow down the pace and the reader's interest. These subtle habits of individual style are discussed in chapter 4.

We started with more than 20,000 extracted features—of which exclamation points and the word "him" were just two—and we studied them all. Some were entailments of style, others offered clues about the plot and setting, and some told us what the books were about. Not all of these features proved to be useful in determining the difference between a novel that had captured a huge number of readers and one that had, despite its unique brilliance, tanked. It turns out, for example, that an author's use of numbers—911, 1984, 867-5309, $1,000,000—has no relationship to sales. Similarly, while we spent a lot of time teaching our machines how to detect that *The Devil Wears Prada* is set in New York City while *Gone Girl* begins in New York but ends up in Missouri, it turns out that (with a few exceptions) the geopolitical setting of a book is not all that important in terms of whether or not it sells well. There were just as many non-bestselling books set in New York as there were bestsellers. The megahit books that are set there—Sylvia Day's *Bared to You,* Tom Wolfe's *The Bonfire of the Vanities*, James Patterson's *The Quickie,* and Safran Foer's *Extremely Loud and Incredibly Close,* to name a few—show a deeper intended or accidental understanding of the minutiae of bestselling DNA than just being set in New York.

In the end, we winnowed 20,000 features down to about 2,800 that were useful in differentiating between stories that everyone seems to want to read and those novels that were more likely to remain, well, niche. After teaching our machines how to read books and extract all of these features, we analyzed the feature set using another batch of computer programs that are designed to discover and learn the latent patterns. Aptly enough, this analysis phase of our study employs something called "machine learning." In text mining, we frequently wish to sort or classify documents according to their similarity. Say, for example, that we want to differentiate between e-mails that are spam and emails that are legitimate correspondence. Because spammy emails tend to have a lot of things in common: misspelled words, a high incidence of the word "Viagra," and so on, we can write programs that measure how likely a given email message is to be a spammy one. The work we are doing in classifying novels is quite similar to the work that your email filter does. Suppose we want to predict whether a new book that we have never seen before is likely to be a bestseller. If we already have a whole lot of books that best-sold (not spam) and another bunch of books that did not sell well (spam), then we can feed all these books to our computer and train it to recognize these two classes by their distinct feature profiles. This is precisely what we did. In fact, we did it three different ways and when we averaged the results we found that 80 percent of the time our machine could guess which books in our corpus were bestsellers and which ones were not.[*]

---

[*] In our very first experiments at Stanford, back in 2008, we had a first run at

That average of 80 percent means that if you randomly selected 50 recent bestsellers and 50 recent non-bestsellers, our machine could correctly identify 40 of the bestsellers as bestsellers, and 40 of the non-bestsellers as non-bestsellers. Of course, this also means that our machine would think that ten of the bestsellers really should not have been bestsellers and that ten of the non-bestsellers should have sold well. When we conducted a series of tests just like this, our machine was very certain that *Pride and Prejudice and Zombies,* for example, was not bestseller material—and, of course, it was a bestseller; our machine got this one wrong. Of course, *Pride and Prejudice and Zombies* is a book that sold at a time when any reference to Austen assured attention (and it likely still does), and when the movie theaters were full of zombie films. The context of the title, then, likely had an out-of-proportion impact on its sales.

Naturally, there were also non-bestselling books that our machine begged us to read, but that's another story.

---

this challenge of classifying bestsellers. We had a corpus of 20,000 novels but far fewer features to analyze: only 505. That big corpus was useful for a certain type of analysis, but the books in that collection had some biases that favored earlier time periods—it contained a lot of nineteenth-century fiction—and what it contained of more recent fiction was biased toward science fiction, romance, and fantasy. Despite these shortcomings, our results were good; we managed classification accuracies between 70 percent and 80 percent.

For this book, we built an entirely new collection that was both more diverse and more current. Our new corpus has just under 5,000 books, and they include a diverse mixture of non-bestselling ebooks and traditional published novels, and just over 500 *NYT* bestsellers.

The Contract

When the two of us discuss new novels, we tend to talk about the relationship between writer and reader in terms of an unwritten contract to fulfill, a contract whose details are hazy but that nevertheless point to the aesthetic, emotional, intellectual, and even ethical reasons behind the choice to read. We thought a lot about all these expectations of a writer as we trained our model in detecting theme, plot, style, and character.

The tacit contract has many implied clauses. If you're a thriller author, for example, you better have a dead body or two, and you better have mastered the heart-racing scene. If you are writing romance, your stories better end, but not start, with a unified, happy couple. Whoever you are, with the rare exception of a new literary wunderkind who is sometimes acceptable at double length, you have got about 350 pages to take us somewhere and bring us back. These are some of the big expectations, and you've seen the vitriol or heartache of the Goodreads reviews when writers don't fulfill them.

With this in mind, dear Reader, we will make our own contract with you very clear. To wit, here are a few clauses.

1. The One

One of the phenomenons of our culture, and of course the book world, is an obsession with ranked lists. This goes far beyond the bestseller list itself. Just this year newspapers and major retailers have run features titled everything from "The Most

Beautiful Settings from Your Favorite Novels," to "The Ten Most Influential Books of All Time," to "Find Your Book Boyfriend." Goodreads users have collectively curated lists of books on all sorts of topics: best books set in space, best Japanese editions, heroes that matter, the best of the tearjerkers. There are thousands of lists, and there is a certain glee to deciding the rankings, to arguing with them, and, of course, to debating the merits of Mr. Darcy versus Christian Grey as a potential date.

Don't think we could resist playing the list-making game. We know that all book people are asked to recommend a favorite novel. When that question comes, responding "I haven't got one" is a death knell of an answer, both to small talk and to your street cred as a professional reader. It's a four-word way to turn out the light in someone's eyes. So we have played this precarious game because we live in a world of *the one*. One *matters*. Number one on the *NYT* list means something different from number ten. Perhaps because of the overwhelming possibilities of choice in the contemporary world, we seem to have a psychological and cultural need for a winner, a king, a god. Pick *one*.

By the end of this book, we will give you our list and our winner—the model's pick for *the* paradigmatic bestseller of the last thirty years.

2. Blind Faith

The next promise of *The Bestseller Code* is that there has been no editorializing of this choice at all. We agreed from the beginning that we would seek not to choose but to explain the choice. In fact, while we knew other works by the writer, neither of us had read "the one" before the computer picked it for us. Of course we pulled it off the shelf instantly, read it in tandem, and laughed together at the unexpected irony. We recommend you don't jump straight to it—every chapter explains a piece of the puzzle—but then we know the temptation of reading the first and last page of a book.

3. No Magic Tea

We are not going to claim that reading this book for the first or even second time is going to turn you into a bestselling fiction writer. This is not a prescriptive "how to" book and comes attached to no guarantee. You will definitely find many tips that neither of us would overlook if we were going to attempt to write a bestselling novel, and it's unlikely either of us would ever submit a novel to an agent any more without doing some computational analysis of the final draft. But part of the beauty of this story is the twist it gives to the old axiom that great writing is a skill that can't be taught. We are more concerned with twists than teaching.

Almost all the writing guides we know—and we have most enjoyed the ones by blockbuster authors like Dean Koontz and Stephen King—offer wisdom on aspects of prose such as style, character, and plot. We will do the same. We hope it will even take you deeper into the DNA of bestselling than any human eye could manage, and it will lay some of that ineffable *je ne sais quoi* of talented writers bare. But it will not give you a formula to apply. This book will tell you a lot about blockbuster DNA, but you won't be able to copy it any more than you can slice off Adam Johnson's fingerprints and type with them on your own hands.

Our belief, while it may be irritating and old-fashioned, is still that if you want to be a bestselling writer then first you have to learn and really appreciate fiction with as many tools as you can. If we can help you with that process, and you become a bestselling novelist, we would love to hear about it. We'd buy your book and no doubt we'd mine it. But please don't complain that you looked for an easy formula to get a million-dollar contract, and we didn't give it to you. Anyone who offers you that is the same person who will offer you overnight weight loss if only you buy their magic tea.

4. The Black Box

This is not a book about algorithms. We will share the key features we extracted, we'll give you the method in broad strokes, but this is not where to go for machine learning or document retrieval or natural language processing. There are many good books on those subjects, but ours is a book about books, mostly bestselling ones.* We hope we will make you think again about

---

* Many of the techniques we used in this book are introduced in Matt's textbook, *Text Analysis with R for Students of Literature*. *Text Analysis with R* offers a basic introduction to text analysis/mining designed for readers with no formal training in computer science. Matt's other book, *Macroanalysis: Digital Methods and Literary History*, provides a deep dive into several methods we employ here, including topic modeling (which we discuss in chapter 2) and stylometry (in chapter 4). For those seeking an even more detailed orientation to the methods that underlie our research, we recommend Christopher Manning, Prabhakar Raghavan, and Hinrich Schutze's *Introduction to Information Retrieval* from

yourself as a reader or writer, about the purposes of fiction, about writers you think you adore or detest, and even about the relationship between humans and machines. We'll give you lots of results and interpretation about where the machine succeeded in finding bestsellers, where it failed, and what it taught us, but our focus is on *Gone Girl* and *The Goldfinch* not *latent Dirichlet allocation* and *named entity recognition*. These sometimes esoteric methods inform the work we have done here, and the work could not have been done without these tools, but they are only the tools by which the story is wrought: the painter does not paint the brush.

Cambridge University Press and Springer's *An Introduction to Statistical Learning* by Gareth James, Daniela Witten, Trevor Hastie, and Robert Tibshirani. Neither is a book for pure beginners, but together they offer a comprehensive and very well written overview of text mining and machine learning.

2

THE **GODPARENTS,** OR, **WHY YOU MUST TAKE TIME** TO **DATE**

When you walk into a bookstore, the first thing you'll see are several tables of recent books on display. As you now know, it is often the case that someone has paid for most, if not all, of those books to be the first ones you see. For that reason they might be a mix of all sorts of writing—literary novels, autobiographies, cookbooks, page-turners. The rest of the store, though, is arranged by category. If you're a novel reader, you know that there is typically a general fiction section that houses classic and contemporary authors alphabetically, and then the genre writers have their own shelves under headings like Romance and Science Fiction. We are so used to this organization of stores and libraries that finding books has become second nature.

The arrangement of books in Barnes & Noble or any online book retailer reflects the belief that the most important aspect of a book to a reader is what it is about. The whole industry is organized around this assumption. Every book that is traditionally published is assigned one or more BISAC (Book Industry Standards and Communication) subject codes. These codes are determined by the Book Industry Study Group, a trade association that is responsible for maintaining industry standards. There are thousands of codes to choose from: in fiction alone there are 152 BISAC codes that determine how a book will be categorized, displayed, and sold, and they get as specific as "historical romance novels with vikings."

There are no similarly important systems of organization for the other aspects of novels that matter to readers—happy endings, tearjerkers, books set in Tokyo, or novels that feature firefighters or princesses or nuns. There is no system to indicate whether the style is minimalist, like Hemingway, or more complex like David Foster Wallace. There's no way of knowing based on how bookstores are arranged if the protagonist is male or female, old or young, or if a story is set in London or Hong Kong.

It should be fair to say, then, that the "what" of a book is considered paramount. If you recommend a book to a friend or if you are a writer yourself and you mention your work, the first question you'll be asked is likely going to be, "What is it about?" It is rarely—unless you are a biographer—*who* is it about, or *where* is it about, or *when* is it about. An interest in subject is what comes first. Which begs the question, what is the killer topic?

Well, our computer thinks there are a few, and so do blockbuster authors. In *On Writing*—one of the most popular recent books by a genre author about the craft of writing—Stephen

King suggests that aspiring novelists take a subject they know and then blend in "personal knowledge of life, friends, relationships, sex and work. Especially work. People love to read about work. God knows why but they do." It's a curious observation about work, telling about our culture, and it turns out that our computer model more or less agrees with King on this one. King is also on fairly safe ground in recommending relationships. When it comes to sex in fiction, though, our machines tell us that King is surprisingly wrong (we will get back to this sex business soon), and neither is he best serving those readers who will take him literally when he suggests that "plumbers in space is not such a bad setup for a story." Don't do it.

Of course King's tone is as entertaining as ever, and somewhat glib, and very consistent with other writers on the subject of theme. Ultimately, though, he is not all that helpful. The brevity of commentary on literary topics from one of the most commercially successful writers of the past hundred years is perhaps to do with one or the other of two stated beliefs. First, he writes that "fiction writers, present company included, don't understand very much about what they do—not why it works when it's good, not why it doesn't when it's bad." This is likely more humble than it is true, but why should an imaginative writer be expected to explicate analytically what might come naturally—in this case the right topics in the right proportions that will appeal to a mass readership all over the world? Second, King writes that to select a theme in a premeditated way with commercial success in mind is "morally wonky." This claim is also likely more humble than it is true. It is hard to believe that the multimillion-dollar authors out there don't think with some savvy about themes that readers will buy, especially when they know just how many copies will be involved in meeting their publishers' expectations. It might also be unfair for King to imply that a deeper understanding of topics that sell, and any attraction to working with them, is morally grey.

Our job here is not to say whether a writer's choices are morally right or wrong. Neither will it be to say that one novel is good and another bad, or one subject is more appropriate or worthy for the pen than any other. We will leave the ethics of creativity to the creatives and the job of judgment to the critics. Our job as literary scholars is simply to bring new explanations, or uncover hidden truths, in the hope of making something once obscure more evident. To do this for the role of theme in literature, we have to become clear about the difference between a topic and a theme, and how both work together to create the unique art that is fiction.

Why Read?

If you think back to your time in high school, where one of the first novels you were asked to read with literary critical eyes was likely *To Kill a Mockingbird* or *Lord of the Flies,* you'll remember that you were meant to notice a difference between topic and theme. Your teacher may have asked some brave person in the classroom to posit an answer to the question of what William Golding's *Lord of the Flies* is about. Ours did—we both have that memory—and it feels like a trick question. Well, we might have ventured, it is about a group of schoolboys who are stranded on an uninhabited tropical island; it is about boys who find ways to organize themselves, survive, and then disband into different factions, one of which is eventually murderous. The topics in the story are English boys, desert islands, hunting, hut-building, and so on. But our teachers wanted something more. What they wanted, having taught us to read more deeply, was that we would observe that the "big" themes of the novel were more latent, more about the human condition, and, possibly, more about what Golding was really trying to communicate with his readership. Along these lines, we might conclude from a study of the assembled topics that *Lord of the Flies* is actually about the nature versus nurture debate, or about good and evil, or friendship, or whether humanity is more inclined, when left alone, to civilization or savagery. If you understood that in English class, then you likely got an A. You might have got an A+ if you explained how Golding's particular choice of topics, mostly made up of common nouns in patterns of repetition, ultimately leads us to see these human truths that he is presenting.

Think some more about why you read the novels you read. The conventional wisdom of the book industry is that you read for theme, and that might seem pretty obvious. That is, until you really start thinking about it. If we ask you what you like to read about, you might say crime or war or sex or fishing. In nonfiction especially, people are driven to books on specific topics: food and business are two perennial favorites. But many fiction readers don't *really* claim to read like that. When we ask people why they chose the last novel they read, they might answer:

"I chose it because it was about the Holocaust."

"I chose it because I was told it was a feel-good read."

"I heard this was a great new literary writer."

"Don't I read *every* Stephen King novel?"

People might also claim they read because of prizes—"I want to read that new Pulitzer from Adam Johnson"—or because they are about to go on vacation to Paris and the novel is set there, or because they have just gone through a breakup and want a weepy love story, or, of course, "because it is a *New York Times* bestseller." We understand that topic is not the only driver of interest in a novel. However, topic is central to the industry and central to the possibilities of a specific story. Therefore, in this chapter we will isolate it and show what a computer is able to do to clarify how it works in bestselling fiction.

The experience of a novel is prompted only by words in different orders, or by certain building blocks of language. Many of these building blocks are nouns, and nouns in different proportions are the vehicle through which authors deliver topic and in turn deliver theme. It is the author's innate sense of proportion and delicate balance of delivery that computers and text mining can help us see, explore, and understand as a part of the overall experience of reading.

The relationship between theme and experience is easy to describe. You might take the example of those tens of thousands of women out there who are devoted to romances, who read constantly, and almost exclusively in that genre. That would be no exaggeration because these readers really do exist in great numbers. When we attended the *Romantic Times* conference last year—a several-day event that is almost enough to convince you that love really does rule the world—we met several huge fans of the genre, fans who swore they personally read three to five *hundred* romance novels per year. How do they do that? We don't know. The superhuman consumption of romance is not the point here. What *is* the point is that popping romance novels like candy kisses, while ostensibly a choice or mild addiction to do with the same topics over and over again, isn't necessarily about picking books by subject. Yes, we expect romance novels to feature some aspect of relationships and love— that's part of the unwritten contract that the romance author is committed to. But romance novels are about all sorts of diverse topics. BISAC has codes for romances about vampires, romances about Scottish people, about Tudors, about sports, about medieval times, and about sex, to name just a few. Perhaps there are some readers out there who are purists, readers who will *only* select romance novels that are also about paranormal shape-shifters (yes, paranormal shifters are a real BISAC category). But isn't it just as likely that some romance readers are in fact reading for a specific kind of *experience,* achieved by the dominance of an abstract theme such as love rather than a more niche topic such as "Western cowboys"? Who cares if the hero is a vampire or a veterinarian so long as he is gorgeous and good?

The bridge between topic and a reader's experience likely can't be stressed enough in a book that is trying to bring to readers some understanding of commercial success. Consider romance alongside thrillers. These are two centrally important categories for any researcher of the contemporary book world because they are the two most lucrative genres. They rule the market, albeit different areas of the market. Thrillers still seem to have more power when it comes to the *New York Times* list. This is especially true in hardback. On the other hand, the rapidly expanding world of self-published ebooks thrives primarily on romance readers and writers. There is lots that could be made of that, enough for a whole other book: train commuters reading spicy novels on iPhones but crime stories in paperback; men and women reading crime in equal proportion, a romance market that is predominantly female. The observation for this book, though, is that romances and thrillers both include topics that create a certain type of mental, imaginative, and emotional experience. A thriller reader, for example, likely buys books whose covers promise themes of torture and spies and alibis because these readers enjoy the emotional experiences of imagined worlds where people are threatened, chased, and murdered. Certainly, thrillers that rouse no sense of fearful suspense are rarely cited as leading examples of the genre. A thriller full of fishing and T-shirt printing is less likely from the outset to drive a book that really works. Just as the romance reader wants love, the thriller novel should show us a dominance of the crime theme. The point is clear: if we want to understand a successful topic in literature, we have to think about what it might do to us and what we want done to us. It must get more specific than the idea of something like King's call, to paraphrase, "to write what you know plus love, sex, work and relationship."

We designed a computer model around the hypothesis that a more granular understanding of topic than the typical human eye might manage would give us deeper insight into the topics seen most frequently on the bestseller list. And it did. You'd think, given all the topics in the world to choose from, that bestselling would turn out to be all about sex, drugs, and rock and roll. But it's not. Far, far from it.

Sex, Drugs, and Rock and Roll

Sex	0.001%
Drugs	0.003%
Rock and Roll	0.001%

Those miniscule percentages reflect the measured presence of sex, drugs, and rock and roll, on average, in the contemporary novels of our research collection. Those tiny percentages are likely so shocking that we will explain them and then shock you again. If we take a cross section of almost five thousand novels—five hundred of which are bestsellers and the rest are not—and measure the presence of five hundred different themes across all of them, then the proportion of the whole taken up by sex is just about a thousandth of a percent. If you then measure the content of bestselling novels (and we will explain how this is done in just a moment), this fraction for sex goes down to 0.0009 percent.

It's hard to believe. Who would have thought that sex does not sell? We tell people and still they do not believe us. But the truth is this: sex, or perhaps more precisely erotica, sells, and it sells in notable quantities, but only within a niche market. Titles within that genre rarely break out enough to win the attention of the mainstream reading market that creates bestsellers. We know what you are thinking: "What about *Fifty Shades of Grey*?" Well, that novel (or those novels if you count the whole series) is one quite rare example of an erotic story that hit the lists. In the next chapter we will offer our explanation for that success, and it has little to do with sex.

Contrary to what you might expect given the prominence of sex in TV, movies, and the media, the U.S. reading public of the past thirty years has demonstrated a preference for other topics. The mix of topics that tend to dominate contemporary bestsellers suggests a reader who wants books to be something different from the lowest common denominator.

But how do we know this?

The linguist John Rupert Firth noted in 1957 that the way to understand a word is by looking at the company it keeps. Put simply, the meaning of a word is found in the context in which it appears. The words "sex," "drugs," and "rock and roll" that appear as the subheading for this section could have been read as synonyms for "gender," "aspirin," and "fun at the beach," but you knew they weren't those things because of the context—each of the nouns in the phrase qualifies the others. Take another example: the word "bar." This simple word will lead us to two important observations about contemporary literature, but taken alone this one word is no use at all. The word *bar* might refer to the exam a trainee lawyer needs to pass, or it may refer to the place he goes to celebrate when the exam has been passed. It might even become a verb: if he goes to the *bar* having passed his *bar* exam and drinks too heavily he may end up being *barred* and even put behind *bars*. The computer has to be trained to understand all this, and this training is all about understanding what Firth said seventy years ago. The machine must learn to look at every word within the context of words that occur in close-by sentences. The algorithmic method for operationalizing this kind of word contextualization on a grand scale is called topic modeling.[*]

The mathematics involved in topic modeling is fairly complicated, but the broad outlines of the process are easy enough to understand. Every novel is a mix of topics and these topics are expressed by words, particularly the nouns. A book about finance will likely include nouns such as "bank," "interest," "money," and "fiduciary." Another book about fishing might include "bank," "river," "fish," and "grass." Both books use the noun "bank," but by looking at the other nouns that tend to occur alongside each occurrence of "bank" inside each book, the algorithm is able to notice repeated patterns and figure out, just like a human reader, that different instances of "bank" have different meanings.[†] Obviously, the word "bank" alone is not a topic, it is only one noun, but when that one

---

[*] In our research we used latent Dirichlet allocation, a topic-modeling algorithm developed by Columbia University Professor, David Blei. The "latent" in Blei's title refers to the topics that are *latent* in a document.

[†] Matt describes more of the detail about how topic modeling works in chapter 8 of his book *Macroanalysis: Digital Methods and Literary History* (UIUC Press, 2013). In chapter 13 of *Text Analysis with R for Students of Literature* (Springer, 2014), he teaches readers how to perform topic modeling in R (and how to make the word clouds used here). Matt's also written several "layman's" explanations on his blog (www.matthewjockers.org) including: "The LDA Buffet is Now Open; or, Latent Dirichlet Allocation for English Majors" (9/29/11) and "'Secret' Recipe for Topic Modeling Themes" (4/12/13).

Fig. 1.

noun is constantly seen alongside other nouns that we recognize as being about financial matters, then we understand that the model has discovered a topic about money. Alternatively, when we encounter "bank" with nouns like "fish" and "river," then we know that the model has discovered a collection of words that signals the presence of a topic about fishing. In the topic modeling we did for this book, one of the topics our machine exposed looked like Figure 1.

This is a topic about bars, specifically the kind you enter in order to enjoy a whiskey, neat. The meaning is straightforward, and in this visualization of the topic the size of the words tells us something about how much more regularly the word "bar" appears in relation to the other words around it. That makes perfect sense. The words around it—"bartender," "drink," "whiskey," "beer"—give us the evidence we need to say with confidence that when the computer finds a cluster of these nouns within the same page or two, the author is writing about a situation in an everyday local bar.

Not all topics that the machine detects are so easy to interpret as this one about bars, and this is where some discernment and knowledge of books comes in. Occasionally we will have to recognize the unusual language of a fantasy series or of novels that are heavy with dialect. A topic composed of invented words such as *nadsat* (teen), *moloko* (milk), and *chepooka* (nonsense) would indeed seem like total *chepooka* if you weren't able to recognize the presence here of some keywords from Anthony Burgess's novel *A Clockwork Orange*. More often than that, though, we might see a topic cloud like Figure 2.

Nouns such as "eyes," "mouth," "hand," and "head" show us that this is about the body. But "the body" alone isn't a sufficient label for this topic. A body could be described in the aftermath of a murder scene, and clearly this is not that. The contextual nouns at the edge of this cloud—"kisses," "pleasure," "smile," "breathing," "bed," "rhythm," and "fire"—tell us that these grouped nouns form a love scene. But a love scene is not just a love scene. They come in all varieties. Most creative writers say that the challenge of writing sex in the right way is not something they particularly look forward to, and each manages it—to greater or lesser effect—with their own style. We have to note, then, that the kind of author who uses the nouns in the

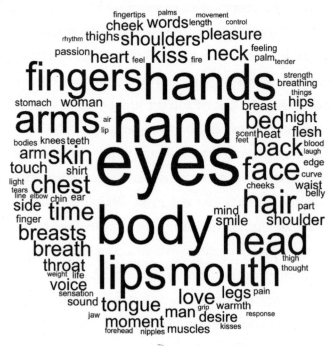

Fig. 2.

word cloud above to write a sex scene is writing a novel with a different sort of sensibility than one who would use much rougher or more graphic language. We have those clouds too, the graphic ones, and the sex scenes they indicate fall somewhere on a scale from something like "what you might read in front of your grandmother" to "what only the strongest stomach can digest."

When we run this topic-modeling algorithm, we get two important pieces of data back. First, the machine tells us which topics exist in our collection and as part of that, which words compose each topic, such as those words seen in the bar and body topics we just discussed. Second, the machine tells us the proportion of each topic in every book. We measured five hundred topics for every novel in our collection, so the possible variations of topical makeup were huge. Once we know those proportions, we can begin to look for patterns that are typical to bestselling books. What the machine does is a kind of reverse engineering. Take the metaphor of a bowl of soup. The machine first separates out all the ingredients—the meat, stock, peppers, onions, and spices—and then it carefully measures how much of each ingredient was used in that favorite recipe.

Once the ingredients are identified in this manner, we are able to ask all kinds of questions. We can begin testing whether bestselling novels are more likely to feature the kind of bank we draw cash from or the kind we sit on by a river. We might ask whether soft or more graphic sex scenes are more likely to hit the lists. If you're interested in those particular questions, by the way, the *NYT* list prefers a bank to have money and sex (when it *does* appear) to suggest intimacy and not aggression. A sex scene will make the list if it moves the plot between characters forward. If it is a gratuitous aside, not needed for storytelling, it likely will not chart and does not need writing. Perhaps this explains why the presence of sex topics diminishes when we compare a large sample of the market with just the top sellers.

Of course, no novelist weaves a tale with just one topic. A book such as Norman Maclean's *A River Runs through It* is, arguably, about fishing *and* monetary matters, but also religion and the relationship between two brothers. Every novel has its own topic profile, which shows not only the topics used to create the thematic experience of the novel, and its particular message, but also the exact proportion in which they appear.

When it comes to bestselling, it turns out that both these things are important to thematic success. Could we know, just from a manuscript, if one topic profile was more likely to hit number one than another?

It may be fair to guess, as many editors do, that a novel about murder, criminal investigations, and team sports is more likely to appeal to the mass American public than one with reptile collecting, space rockets, and college classrooms. But to create a real prediction, you have to ask yourself if there are topics that not just a few but *many* of the bestsellers have in common, and, at the same time, you have to know if these are topics that are less likely to occur in novels that never hit the lists. It's a complicated problem to solve. A glance at the novels on the list for any given week would seem to suggest a random assortment of topics without any common threads at all.

Take the current bestseller list. At the time of writing, number one on the hardback list in fiction is John Grisham with his new novel *Rogue Lawyer*. That might be no huge surprise since Grisham novels and the number one slot go together like potato salad and the Fourth of July. The open question, though, is whether or not that position on the list has anything to do with his choice of topics. Number two on the list is a James Patterson detective novel featuring Alex Cross. Three is a Tom Clancy written by someone else (since the author died in 2013). Then we have stories by Stephen King, a crime novel by David Baldacci, a love story by Nicholas Sparks, and one of Janet Evanovich's ongoing series about a female bounty hunter. So far all these novels would be considered genre fiction, although in different genres. King's book, being a collection, likely has more topical diversity than a coherent novel, and we might guess that his topics, as a horror and suspense writer, are in any case quite different from those of James Patterson. Next we have the Pulitzer Prize–winning novel *All the Light We Cannot See,* then a new mystical and musical tale from the typically spiritual writer Mitch Albom. Paula Hawkins follows with *The Girl on the Train* (for the forty-seventh week), then the new/old Harper Lee novel *Go Set a Watchman,* followed by a detective story from Michael Connelly, *The Nightingale* by Kristen Hannah (which like *All the Light We Cannot See* is set in WWII), a Danielle Steel romance, and one of the novels by George R. R. Martin.

Given those books, what is the hardback bestseller list about? Apparently it is about nothing in particular and everything in particular. But there are patterns. A clue here, if you are thinking about the problem, is that George R. R. Martin is a bit of a red herring. His current bestseller status at the end of 2015 is likely thanks to the massive success of the HBO series *Game of Thrones.* His is the one novel so far that, topically at least, is the unlikely bestseller. Thirty years ago his topics would have been spot on, but nowadays contemporary realism is more in vogue.

We are writing this the week before Christmas, which means that veteran big-name authors will be dominating the list because of holiday gifts, so the game of pattern recognition is a lot easier to play than in other weeks of the year. It would seem that the dominant topic on the list is crime. A secondary topic is war, which is perhaps the elder brother of crime. While we may want to presume the topic of love for Sparks and Steel, brief descriptions of their two novels suggest threatening relationships and the death of a beloved man. Not necessarily so upbeat. King, if he is still the Stephen King he always was, has written something scary and suspenseful. And so on. Perhaps, regardless of the reasonably (but not very) diverse topics on the list this week, we might conjecture that the themes most likely to chart are violence and fear. From that, our two-minute analysis might end with the conclusion that in studying this fascinating cultural construct called the *NYT* bestseller list, we have learned that the contemporary American public has an obsession with violence that could keep psychiatrists and sociologists busy for some time.

Well, neither of us is about to refute that insight, and neither of us is a trained sociologist, either. We'll just leave it there, as a possibility, but before you register yourself as a new literary agent who picks winners by picking violence, we'll encourage some deeper attention to the patterns latent in these books and in this list.

It only takes a glance at the trade paperback list for this same week to consider some backtracking. Of the top ten books, only one is ostensibly about crime. It is another James Patterson, this one about when Alex Cross is called away from a family Christmas into a hostage situation. In fact, there is no obviously dominant topic on the paperback list at all. Top is *The Martian*, about living on Mars, whose sales have been affected greatly by the Matt Damon movie. Second is an old Philip K. Dick novel, sort of a Second World War novel, only in this one we see what may have happened if the Allies had lost. There are a couple of novels in a series about women, love, and friendship. Paulo Coehlo's *The Alchemist*, an allegory about a journeying shepherd, deserves mention for being on the list, to date, for a massive 383 weeks. In Ernest Cline's *Ready Player One,* set in 2044, the protagonist is jacked into a virtual utopia. It is another book with a movie on the way. Four novels—Dick's novel, then *Everything I Never Told You,* then *Orphan Train,* then *Brooklyn*—are all set in different decades of the twentieth century. So perhaps it is not violence but history that is the signal of mega-success? If so, it seems a rather weak one. Four books is not ten. Thinking deeper now, perhaps, on second thought, the overarching theme for this list is journeying?

Not much is very clear so far other than that in December 2015, no character on the bestseller list was having a very good time. But pattern recognition is about observation and testing. So for the fun of it we might say that the multimillion-dollar book deal, from first glance at the lists on this random day, should come for a novel about a fearful or violent journey. We might say that would be a good bet for today's market. And of course that leaves your editor fairly free, because a fearful journey might be a romance, might be a thriller, could be a literary novel, and could even be sci-fi. Many writers could take the assignment of a fearful journey and have it lead to their own particular message, which is why all bestsellers feel different, but in some sense we will find that they are quite the same.

One important thing to take away from this quick glance at one week's list is that topic transcends genre. The first thing to do if you want to write, publish, or predict a bestseller is to forget the whole notion of genre that dominates the industry. Marriage can show up in any genre. So, too, can love and crime. The proportions of these topics in the different genres may be different, but the presence of key topics somewhere within a manuscript of any kind does matter. All the work we have done has told us that genre is usually a straitjacket: forget it. If you are willing to grasp this way of thinking, then you have started to think like a computer in search of a predictive model.

Validation

Every book in our collection is given a percentage score for the presence of five hundred topics. Of course, some topics may not appear in some books—there are no cowboys in *The Da Vinci Code*. But for every manuscript we do get something that looks like the bar graph on the next page, which shows only the top five topics in Jodi Picoult's novel *House Rules*: 23 percent of her book deals with a topic we call "Kids and School," 10 percent is about "Crime Scenes," 7 percent deals with "Courtrooms and Legal Matters," 6 percent involves "Domestic Settings," and 2 percent is engaged with "Close Relationships."

Once the topic-modeling algorithm has figured out what the major topics are, and once it has cataloged and quantified where and to what extent they appear in every book, we feed a randomly selected subset of the results to a machine-learning algorithm that knows in advance which books in the subset were the bestsellers and which ones were not. Because the machine already knows which books are which, it creates a profile of which topics in what proportions we are most likely to encounter when picking up a bestseller. And even more than that, the machine is able to identify which topics are used most

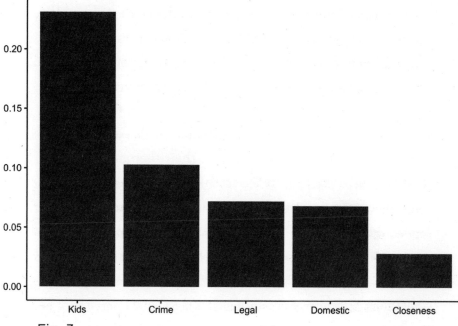

Top Five Topics in Jodi Picoult's House Rules

Fig. 3.

differently. The sex topic that we wrote about earlier is a good example. On average, that topic appears twice as often in non-bestsellers as it does in bestsellers. The machine is able to detect that difference and then use what it has learned to aid it in making predictions about whether an unidentified manuscript is likely to sell well or not. According to our model, a book with sex in almost every chapter is less likely to hit the lists. There are exceptions to this, of course—who can ignore Sylvia Day or E. L. James?—but two authors alone cannot overly influence a whole model, which is examining thousands of books.

Ultimately, our machine was able to use the topical data to

correctly guess whether or not a book in our collection was a bestseller 80 percent of the time.* And when we asked the trained model which authors of the past thirty years have the best understanding (practiced or instinctive) of getting the right topics in the right proportions, it gave us two names: John Grisham and Danielle Steel. We were stunned. Our reaction wasn't so much a comment about their work—at this point, we still had to look more closely at their thematic DNA. Instead, it was a reaction to the fact that the model had picked two of the most successful living writers of all time. Of all their books, the topic model selected several for the top of the list. The favorites from Steel were *The House on Hope Street*, *Mixed Blessings*, and *The Accident*. From Grisham, they were *The Litigators*, *The Associate*, and *Calico Joe*.

---

* This measure of accuracy is derived using a process called cross-validation. In this case, we employed two types of cross-validation, which, to satisfy those readers who follow the technicalities, first involved repeatedly training on a randomly selected 90 percent of the books and then testing the model on the remaining 10 percent. In a second test, we used a "hold one out" approach in which we trained a series of models while holding out just one book at a time. In both experiments, we know we are doing well if the machine correctly guesses the class (bestseller or non-bestseller) of the held-out book, or books in the case of the first test. It is a rigorous process that involves training and testing many models. When training these models we have to use books that are already published, and books that we already know to be bestsellers or not. The first model we built was in 2011. When we added all the bestsellers and more non-bestsellers from the last five years to our library, we were able to test the model yet again and in a sense see if the observations of 2011 persisted into 2015. They did. Once cross-validation has given us confidence, we can examine the predictions and the associated probabilities for every book. Some books the model is not certain about at all, and these might get a score of only 51 percent certainty. Considering a random chance guess would be 50/50, that is not very confident. In that case, we would want to investigate all the other qualities of the manuscript—style, perhaps, or plotlines, before making any comment on its likely success. But other books the model predicts with a great deal of confidence, and it ranks them accordingly.

Likely Heroes

We have come to refer to Danielle Steel and John Grisham as "the godparents" of the contemporary bestseller partly because for the past several decades they have been long-standing guardians of the list. Their shared output is huge, their commitment is inspirational, their performance is unquestionable. The resulting wealth of the godparents would likely be sufficient to launch the careers of a hundred or even a thousand young writers. We also call them the godparents because in the writing world they are two possible role models who seem to protect, embody, and live the American Dream.

Certainly, to read about their lives is not too far from reading about the lead character of a deftly plotted paperback page-turner. Danielle Fernandes Dominique Schuelein-Steel was born in 1947 in New York City, an only child. Her father was part of a wealthy beer dynasty; her mother the beautiful daughter of a Portuguese diplomat. As a young child, she was exposed to the wild dinners and lifestyles of the rich and glamorous and began writing stories and poems. When she was only seven, her parents divorced, and she was raised in Paris and New York, mostly by her father, servants, and other relatives. She saw very little of her mother. Steel enrolled in design school with a dream of becoming a couture designer. Her passion was thwarted by high pressure to achieve and a resulting stomach ulcer. At age eighteen, she married the first of several wealthy and powerful men, and her marriage brought her a privileged lifestyle and multiple homes. She wanted to work, and started a career in PR and advertising, where one of her clients suggested she consider writing. In the early 1970s she retreated into her San Francisco home to write her first novel. When she recounts this tale, she recalls late nights writing in the laundry room on top of the washing machine so as not to wake the family.

John Ray Grisham Jr. was born in 1955 in Arkansas. His father was a construction worker who took John and his four siblings around the South to wherever there was work. Neither of his parents had the opportunity of a college degree, and the family, who settled in Mississippi when he was twelve, was not monied. Like Steel, Grisham had a dream career that was not writing. His major talent in high school was sports, and he was a star in baseball. He fostered the hope of a professional sports career until he counseled himself to walk away and study accounting and then tax law. Grisham became a street lawyer—an attorney who represents individuals and not corporations—married a childhood friend to whom he is still married, and had two children. He had no intention of becoming a novelist until he started the practice of watching the court cases of better-paid lawyers. One day, he sat and listened to the testimony of a ten-year-old girl who had been raped and left for dead. The emotion and drama of the story was immensely powerful to him, and he began to wonder what would have happened if the girl's father murdered the rapist as an act of revenge. He wondered what would happen in the South if the rapist was white and the avenging father was black. Obsessed with the story, he challenged himself to write it down, to see if he could manage a work of fiction. For three years he woke at 5

A.M. every day to write before starting his seventy-hour work-week as a lawyer.

Are these two author bios not like a précis for a star-studded heroine and a blockbuster hero? They almost *had* to make it! Of course, neither author had an overnight rise to stardom. Several decades later both, when interviewed, noted the importance of hard work, persistence, and tenacity. This, after all, was the American Dream.

Published in 1973, Steel's first book, *Going Home,* sold fairly quickly, but she wrote five more novels, working eighteen to twenty hours a day, that she could not find a publisher for. Determined not to give up, she finally sold the seventh. Her second novel to market was published in 1977. Since then, she has given us almost a hundred more, alongside children's books and nonfiction, and not one has not been a bestselling book.

Grisham's manuscript that followed from watching the rape case, first titled *Deathknell* and later *A Time to Kill,* was rejected by many agents and editors before David Gernert, the last in a long line of would-be Grisham agents, managed to sell it to the twenty-sixth publisher he tried. Grisham got a contract for $15,000 with a print run of 5,000. Few of the books sold: Grisham himself is rumored to have bought a thousand of them. But Grisham kept writing, and *The Firm* was his second effort. The film rights for that story sold first, for $600,000. The novel sold shortly after for $200,000. Since it was published, in 1991, it has made around a hundred appearances on the bestseller lists.

Both Steel and Grisham fast became regulars on the lists, and have stayed there year-on-year since the start of their careers. Depending on which statistics you want to believe, and which statistic you favor, both of them have the most impressive sales of any author alive. Steel is often cited as the fourth-bestselling writer of all time, after Shakespeare, Agatha Christie, and Barbara Cartland. Across her roughly 130 books, she has published in 69 countries and 43 languages. She reached the *Guinness Book of World Records* in 1989 for having a book on the *NYT* list for 381 weeks. Since she started her career, she is estimated to have sold six hundred million copies.

Grisham has a much smaller backlist of thirty-five novels, but early in his career he achieved an unprecedented four books in the top spots at once—number one in hardback and numbers one, two, and three in paperback. That achievement meant that Grisham was at that time labeled the fastest-selling novelist in publishing history. He has single-handedly dominated the number one spot in *Publishers Weekly*'s annual chart of the best-selling book of the year ever since he started writing. In the 1990s, he sold almost 61 million books. Steel sold 37.5 million that decade.

Whichever of them, ultimately, will maintain their name in brighter lights, we think you'll agree on the basic point: They have both made it in novel writing. They have *seriously* made it.

But why?

Clearly there is something compelling and significant in the fact that a computer read several thousand contemporary novels, equally blind to the status of every author, and picked Danielle Steel and John Grisham as two authors most likely to succeed based on their understanding of theme and topic. The odds seem unfeasibly small. The number of possible combinations of possible topics in all these different novels is truly enormous. How could it be that an algorithm chose two of the handful of authors who have been so stratospherically successful in the past thirty years?* Was the stratospheric success of Steel and Grisham always written into the DNA of their manuscripts? The answer is likely yes. But another curious question is how come these ostensibly very different writers were grouped together by an algorithm? Despite the fact one writes thrillers and the other romances, they must be doing some topical things the same way.

If we compute an average proportion for each topic in all the books by each of these authors, it certainly seems that Steel and Grisham learned something from the old maxim "write what you know." The author who dreamed of baseball but then became an attorney has "Lawyers and the Law" as his most prevalent theme, followed by "American Team Sports." Steel, who has been through five marriages, raised nine children and lost one, writes mostly about "Domestic Life," "Love," and "Maternal Roles." While Steel in particular claims to write about a very diverse set of themes—the World Wars, Wall Street, the fashion industry, illness, siblings, embezzlement, abortion—it turns out this apparent diversity is in small proportion. The topical data reveal that each of the godparents has one topic that is overwhelmingly important to their brand, and

---

* For those who care about such things, some details of how we controlled for multiple books by the same author are provided in the postscript.

there is much computational evidence to support that this kind of focus is a wise approach.

If a reader enters an implied contract when they pick up a favorite writer's book, part of the expectation is topical. Both Grisham and Steel consistently deliver this, and in the same proportions. Roughly a third of all the paragraphs Grisham has ever written deal directly with the legal system, and similarly Steel has given almost an exact mathematical third of her pages over the years to the theme of domestic life, or even more specifically "time spent inside the home." There are several significant things to say here. The authors are known for their signature topic, and fans expect them to deliver it. If that trademark gets a third of the book, the book-per-year writer then has two-thirds of his or her space to introduce the tangential topics that make each new book seem a little different. This formula can go on forever, and we will see how cleverly this is done: for now the point is in the proportion—one-third the same, two-thirds different.

We investigated this a little further, and found an interesting pattern across all our bestselling books, beyond just Steel and Grisham. It turns out that successful authors consistently give that sweet spot of 30 percent to just one or two topics, whereas non-bestselling writers try to squeeze in more ideas. To reach a third of the book, a lesser-selling author uses at least three and often more topics. To get to 40 percent of the average novel, a bestseller uses only four topics. A non-bestseller, on average, uses six. While this may sound like a lot of numbers, the effect on your reading experience and the cohesion of a satisfying narrative is quite significant. Telling the heart of a story with fewer topics implies focus. It implies lack of un-needed subplots. It implies a more organized and precise writ-erly mind. It implies experience.

We tested this finding with two of our friends—an agent and a novelist. Both told us that they had, through a series of painful rejections from publishing houses, come to the theory that new writers start out too ambitious. They said such writ-ers tend to favor the approach of telling a complex situation from all angles, which will entail many topics. Writers are ob-servers, and it is natural for them to want to share all that they have observed about the human condition. While writing such a topic-rich novel can be a very satisfying intellectual endeavor, the market tends to reject it. It's too much in a 350-page expe-rience. Focus that brings both depth and a story that can be easily followed is the preference—topics in fiction are not meant to amount to an encyclopedia. They serve as the under-lying linchpins for character and emotional experience and are meant to overshadow neither.

Grisham and Steel each have only one signature theme, not two, that takes up a whole third (on average) of each of their novels. This likely helps with their branding. All the many other topics each writer employs are used in tiny percentages. Grisham's second-most-used topic across his canon is American sports, but it is the subject of only 4 percent of his pages, and this average is no doubt as large as it is because it gets a big bump from his non-legal thriller *Calico Joe*—a book that is en-tirely set in a world of baseball. Many of Grisham's other sec-ondary themes are no big surprise: money (3 percent), cops (2 percent), and government intelligence (2 percent). The less immediately obvious topic, at almost 4 percent of all of Grisham's pages, is a topic we call "everyday moments." The name is deliberately vague and undramatic. The scenes in which this topic shows up prominently may involve two people chatting, or sitting on a sofa watching TV, or walking down the street. Not much is going on but day-to-day living. Its presence as number three in Grisham, after law and sports, is important if only to indicate a writer who is aware of pace. Everyday interactions between characters are there in order to vary the pace of the drama and avoid melodrama. It is the kind of topic no one would likely think they read for, but if these scenes that offer breath and reflection are totally absent, a reader is almost guaranteed to complain.

There are other minor topics in Grisham, though, ones that we would have been less likely to guess immediately. These topics, with similar proportions to cops and courts, deal with people in their domestic environments (a top topic for Steel), kids enjoying summer at home (with words like "porch" and "bike"), scenes about relationships (also very important in Steel), and family.

Steel's top few themes appear to put her characters and those of Grisham in very different worlds. After time spent in the home—a topic whose specific nouns suggest the home of a typical nuclear family—she gives 5 percent more of her storytelling to a similar theme we called "family time." The nouns in this word group suggest a family at home, engaged in everyday activities: dinner, conversation, rest, love, weekends. So far it is all quite low drama. Her third most used topic, though, deals with hospitals and medical care. This topic is made up of words like "nurses," "doctors," "ambulance," "emergency," and "accident." It suggests not the long-term stay of a patient with a chronic disease, but instead the sudden and unexpected event that threatens the domestic contentment of Steel's primary themes. This topic takes up 13 percent of *The Kiss*, 12 percent of *The Accident*, and 8 percent of *The House on Hope Street*—three of the novels that fans often score most highly in online forums dedicated to her work.

This juxtaposition of the family at home and the emergency room is important, and it is reversed in Grisham but to similar effect. Remember, after the legal world Grisham gives us things like kids at home and scenes of relationship. Think of the fuel for story in these juxtapositions, in their implied conflict. The hospital and the court are places of drama, of threat (imaginary or real) to the everyday person. For the average reader, accidents and lawsuits are two things we fear, and two things that may threaten those things we hold dear. Don't we instantly feel protective of these imaginary families? It's human nature to want to know what will happen. Will everyone be all right? How?

What the godparents are teaching us about bestselling is that there must be a dominant topic to give the glue to a novel, and that topics in the next highest proportions should suggest a direct conflict that might be quite threatening. It is not good to have randomly different topics that have as much to do with one another as chalk and cheese—a primary theme of sexuality and a secondary one of gardening, for example, does not imply the same potential human drama that may make for a compelling narrative. Bestselling authors pick combinations with guaranteed hooks—how about children and guns, faith and sex, or love and vampires. (Likely all three combinations have hit the lists.)

The third point to make about bestselling narrative in the current era is realism. The topics we have so far encountered have nothing to do with fantasy. They are not faraway topics for people who are nothing like us. A clever novelist knows the topics that likely already affect the psyche of masses of readers, and they manipulate that knowledge. At least one of the top few of a novel's topics should be something that lots of different people—of different ages, different genders, different cultures—fear. Perhaps our two-minute hypothesis about fearful journey novels was not so bad after all.

The final significant lesson to take from Grisham and Steel on the subject of topic is all about the mainstream. To sell a million copies, a book's topical profile must have the potential to appeal to a mainstream audience. Perhaps you are a reader or writer who prefers the flavor and interest of something fresh and unusual, something like the Swedish politics in Larsson's *The Girl with the Dragon Tattoo* or the art history in Dan Brown or the world of high fashion in *The Devil Wears Prada*. These are good topics, but the data tells us that these should be secondary in terms of proportion to topics of a more universal appeal.

Part of the DNA of Grisham's success is his topic profile of mainstream themes. The same is true for Steel. Grisham's topic of the law has coincided with the rise of the trial as a cultural phenomenon, and with the overuse of the phrase "see you in court." The law court is the contemporary battleground for all the social classes, and it is the arena the public turns up to in order to witness the major cultural and ethical wars of our time: women's equality, race relations, gay marriage, corporate social responsibility, the environment. Think of the massive publicized cases, televised trials, and the shifting of personal responsibility and peacemaking from the accountable individuals to the faceless system of the law. The legal system in the U.S. has also been depicted as the great equalizer: how the public have delighted in the police mugshots of the rich and famous, but it is similarly, endlessly, accused of corruption. The law is, therefore, a wonderful contemporary topic, whether or not you have the storytelling ability of John Grisham, because it contains its own contradiction: the promise of fairness and the promise of threat. It is a perfect topic to take us to some of the larger and more pertinent themes of our era.

Grisham has spoken in many interviews about being very careful not to alienate swathes of readers by being too political in his narratives. While he is an open Democrat, he has reflected that *The Pelican Brief,* for one, was too political, and that he tries if possible to keep his novels inoffensive to people over a wider political spectrum than his own. This likely explains the almost total absence from both his and Steel's topic profiles of topics such as worship, witches, hard drugs, and graphic sex. Emotional and ethical topics are heavily favored, but inflammatory topics are kept to a minimum. A novel is not a soapbox, and neither is being offensive the best strategy for repeated million-dollar book deals. Why offend if it's not really necessary? There are more sophisticated things to do with emotion.

Danielle Steel, who knows just the topics that tweak emotions, ostensibly writes about all sorts of things. But if you read several of her books in a row, what they tend to have in common is a woman who is navigating a modern world in which she could, theoretically and potentially, have it all. Steel's women are often challenged with managing both situations of personal choice that previous generations of women may not have had, and the impact of emotionally grueling circumstances beyond their control. They think hard about their decisions concerning having a career, having children, marrying, and so on, and Steel has tackled surrogacy, abortion, competition, career girls, stay-at-home mothers, divorce, and affairs. In that, she has found both a culturally relevant theme to keep exploring—the choices of the modern woman—and opportunities to keep new novels coming by choosing a new secondary topic.

Still, none of this quite explains why Steel and Grisham came out together on top of our model's list. The model showed us that both authors use many similar minor topics, and they both avoid other topics altogether. There are too many of these to give space to them all, but suffice to say that their common DNA is largely about creating realism and relatability with topics as commonplace as parents, breakfast, and nighttime, and that both avoid with consistency topics such as snakes, wizards, caves, and orcs.

But perhaps the most interesting similarity between Grisham and Steel is that their top-shared topic also happens to be the topic our model found most useful in identifying bestsellers. What that means is not that it is the most common topic among bestselling writers, since those topics may also be common in non-bestsellers. Instead, it is the topic that is most overrepresented in bestselling books when compared to non-bestsellers, and thus it has considerable predictive power. Put more bluntly, it is a topic that writers would do well not to ignore. The topic is deceptively simple, perhaps even mundane, when seen against the backdrop of bold topics such as sex and crime. It is a topic that is indicative to scenes of human interaction and relationships, but we need to be more specific than that. It's not as heady as romantic love, or passion, and neither is it the typical relationship between teacher and class or employer and boss. It is more specifically about human closeness and human connection. Scenes that display this most important indicator of bestselling are all about people communicating in moments of shared intimacy, shared chemistry, and shared bonds.

Steel, a romance writer, is very keen on these scenes, but even Grisham allows his workaholic lawyers such moments of human closeness and bonding. In *The Associate*, Grisham's young lawyer takes an evening off, picks up Chinese takeout and a bottle of wine, and takes it to the house of the woman he is closest to. It's no big "I love you" moment; just more of a casual, easy kind of date where they talk about life and fall asleep on the sofa. In *The Firm*, a different young lawyer does exactly the same thing, also with Chinese food and perhaps the same red wine. It is a staple that works. Characters must have these moments of casual intimacy and closeness, if not explicitly romantic. Be it a shopping date with Mom, a fishing date with Dad, or a cooking date with a new lover, there must be time to date.

Perhaps it is fair to speculate that the portion of the American public that actually reads fiction likes to read more or less about itself. To us, it seems like readers enjoy seeing their own possible realities dramatized. We'll look at topical patterns of the whole market and let you decide.

Two notable sets of underperforming topics are all things fantastical and otherworldly. Made-up languages, fantasy creatures, settings that don't exist, space battles, and starships are all statistically far less likely to succeed on a mass scale than the topics of realism in today's market. Still, in the many topics that suggest a realistic world, there are some that are winners and others that are losers. Among the good, the popular, and (for writers) the go-for-its: marriage, death, taxes (yes, really). Also technologies—preferably modern and vaguely threatening technologies—funerals, guns, doctors, work, schools, presidents, newspapers, kids, moms, and the media. By contrast, among the bad and unpopular, we already have sex, drugs, and rock and roll. To that add seduction, making love, the body described in any terms other than in pain or at a crime scene. (These latter two bodily experiences, readers seem to quite enjoy.) No also to cigarettes and alcohol, the gods, big emotions like passionate love and desperate grief, revolutions, wheeling and dealing, existential or philosophical sojourns, dinner parties, playing cards, very dressed up women, and dancing. (Sorry.)* Firearms and the FBI beat fun and frivolity by a considerable percentage. The reading public prefers to see the stock market described more so than the human face. It likes a laboratory over a church, spirituality over religion, and college more than partying. And, when it comes to that one, big, perennially important question, the readers are clear in their preference for dogs and not cats.

When it comes to place, we also know what we like and we stick to it. The preferred place of action is a town or a city and readers will accept a vast variety of either. We don't like the imagination stretched too far. No to planets other than ours (Andy Weir broke the rule with *The Martian*, but that book is nicely full of laboratory levels of scientific detail, and technologies, and unlike other books set in space, its priority is getting the lead character safely home). The desert is no good, neither is the ocean, neither is the jungle, and neither is a fancy ranch. Better to stick to the average home. Writers, don't take your reader further than you personally have ever been, and if you have been further than most of us, then keep it for your memoir.

Characters we will come to in chapter 5. But the topic model already tells us a few things. Stick to real people. No dwarfs, no lords, no warriors, no priestesses, no sergeants, no dukes, and no wizards (there will only ever be one Harry).

Finally, no unicorns.

---

* Obviously, many people will be able to think of that *one* bestseller that has a dinner party and dancing in it. But one-off cases do not constitute a significant pattern. To hold predictive power, a topic must show up many times on the lists.

The Lists: Theme

Everyone loves a list. These top tens are generated by the bestseller-ometer. Here it only considers thematic data.

Top ten novels based on topical mix (excluding John Grisham and Danielle Steel)

1. Jodi Picoult, *House Rules*
2. Jodi Picoult, *Nineteen Minutes*
3. Janet Evanovich, *Twelve Sharp*
4. David Baldacci, *The Hit*
5. Janet Evanovich, *Plum Lovin'*
6. Dave Eggers, *The Circle*
7. Jodi Picoult, *Handle with Care*
8. Janet Evanovich, *Explosive Eighteen*
9. Janet Evanovich, *Notorious Nineteen*
10. Jodi Picoult, *Sing You Home*

Top ten books with the highest proportion of the bestselling theme of Human Closeness (excluding John Grisham and Danielle Steel)

1. Nora Roberts, *The Last Boyfriend* (38 percent)
2. Sylvia Day, *Entwined with You* (34 percent)
3. Nora Roberts, *Vision in White* (34 percent)
4. Sylvia Day, *Reflected in You* (32 percent)
5. Nora Roberts, *Happy Ever After* (32 percent)
6. Nora Roberts, *Bed of Roses* (32 percent)

7. Nora Roberts, *The Next Always* (31 percent)

8. Sylvia Day, *Bared to You* (31 percent)

9. Emily Giffin, *Love the One You're With* (25 percent)

10. Nora Roberts, *The Hollow* (24 percent)

For the fun of it, here are a few more lists:

Top ten books with the theme of Books and Reading

1. Elizabeth Kostova, *The Historian*

2. Geraldine Brooks, *People of the Book*

3. Umberto Eco, *The Name of the Rose*

4. Ann Shaffer, *The Guernsey Literary and Potato Peel Pie Society*

5. Nicholas Sparks, *True Believer*

6. Deborah Harkness, *A Discovery of Witches*

7. Richard Paul Evans, *The Christmas Box*

8. Eleanor Browne, *The Weird Sisters*

9. Paulo Coelho, *The Alchemist*

10. Bernhard Schlink, *The Reader*

Top ten books with Modern Technology

1. Michael Connelly, *The Burning Room*

2. Patricia Cornwell, *Scarpetta*

3. Dave Eggers, *The Circle*

4. Janet Evanovich, *Twelve Sharp*

5. Stephen King, *Mr. Mercedes*

6. Tim LaHaye and Jerry Jenkins, *The Mark*

7. James Patterson, *Double Cross*
8. James Patterson, *Alex Cross, Run*
9. James Patterson, *Hope to Die*
10. Maria Semple, *Where'd You Go, Bernadette*

Top ten books with Dogs

1. W. Bruce Cameron, *A Dog's Purpose*
2. Nora Roberts, *The Search*
3. Dean Koontz, *The Darkest Evening of the Year*
4. Garth Stein, *The Art of Racing in the Rain*
5. Stephen King, *Cujo*
6. Nicholas Sparks, *The Lucky One*
7. Dean Koontz, *Dragon Tears*
8. Stephen King, *Four Past Midnight*
9. David Wroblewski, *The Story of Edgar Sawtelle*
10. Nicholas Sparks, *The Choice*

THE **SENSATIONS,** OR, **HOW** TO **FORM SOME** PERFECT CURVES

"Excuse the hyperbole," wrote author M. Christian, "but there really are moments when everything just . . . changes: the wheel, the internal combustion engine, antibiotics, the personal computer." And one book. *That* book. "This book," he wrote, "will, no doubt, be remembered as when *everything changed.*" People who hadn't picked up a book in years read this one. Writers in the same genre suddenly found they could make a career. Publishing houses added new editors and imprints, all searching to capitalize on the moment. This was big. Women all over the world discussed its content in the press, on personal blogs, and no doubt with their husbands. It was 2011. *That book* would sell 125 million copies in its first four years.

It was controversial. Reviewers, other writers, and "book people" liked to say it was terrible. Its author was attacked for poor writing skills, bad style, misrepresentation of major themes, immature and unlikely characters, and for failing to understand plotting. On Goodreads, some readers were outraged—to them its author had done a severe disservice not just to literature but to the advancement of women. Comments among the one-star reviews said it "truly exemplifies the meaning of terrible" and "this book is so bad that I feel the need to warn others." But the book caught like a fever. A bookseller in New Jersey, who like every other bookseller was selling every copy she had available, was bemused: "Our customers are very smart and they say it's badly written, but they are in the middle of book three." She got straight to the point. Even the intelligent bookworms who typically favored prize winners and beautiful prose were addicted. They complained about it but wanted more.

The book was *Fifty Shades of Grey*. Literary cocaine to millions of readers, and a problem (initially at least) to two literary scholars who had the book land on their desks with a yellow Post-it attached: "Explain this!"

Treasure Hunting

In our office, we didn't record the exact exchange between us when *Fifty Shades* became the phenomenon it did, but it might have been something like "Uh-oh . . ." from one of us, and "Oh, hell!" from the other. The press had picked up on the first results of our work—the initial three-year study at Stanford—and we had just given an interview claiming that novels packed full of sex are really unlikely to hit the *NYT* list. Then came a novel with sex in practically every chapter, and not just sex, but whips, chains, and floggers—"kinky fuckery" as Anastasia calls it—and everyone in the world, it seemed, wanted to read it.

Everyone had a reaction to *Fifty Shades of Grey*—including millions of people who never read it—and ours (professionally at least) was that we had to test the model and reinvestigate our claims about sex in bestselling novels. The book was a challenge to us, a beckon toward deeper algorithmic understanding of fiction and what turns readers on. Could we have ever seen this coming or was it an anomaly?

As you know, every manuscript we feed the bestseller-ometer receives a score that indicates whether or not it belongs in the bestseller club. Back in 2011, we were working only with computational reading of theme and style. Our standard is high, and while some people might look at our data and be happy to publish a book with a 70 percent score and aim to maximize its chances with brilliant publishing and marketing, in evaluating our model, we have tended to see scores as satisfactory only when the machine returns a number over 95 percent.

We fed *Fifty Shades of Grey* to the algorithms, unsure about whether it was about to break the whole system. How would the model appraise this new kind of freak bestseller, about Ana and Christian and their adventures in the BDSM playroom? As it happens, the algorithms were not entirely flummoxed. They had things to show us.

Our original theme and style model (and we will get to style in the next chapter) gave E. L. James a score of 90 percent. What that score told us was that there had to be something more to this book than kinky sex. Because the model had been trained on a corpus of books that included many erotic novels that had not hit the lists, it rightfully correlated explicit sexual content with poor chances of hitting the *New York Times*. Based on long-standing and established patterns of success, the model had learned to associate topics like kinky sex and BDSM with a low probability of big market success. The model is not a crystal ball for the next "buzz topic," and yet, it seemed to see something in this new book.

Despite the furor, perhaps kinky sex *wasn't* the best explanation for its success. If it really were true that *Fifty Shades* sold simply because everyone wants to read "mommy porn" (as the press dubbed the novel), then the algorithm would have been way off. What we saw instead was that while our model did not particularly favor E. L. James's writing style (only about 50/50 as a measure of potential success), it still told us she had got something in her topical makeup just about right. How could that be?

Well, in the previous chapter we explained that most best-selling novels have two or three themes that together make up about a third of a novel, and that writers (especially those who write similar books year after year) might add smaller percentages of other topics to give their readers variation and flavor. We said that there are several topics, such as twenty-first-century technologies, that are overrepresented in contemporary bestsellers compared to novels that tend not to sell in big numbers. The top differentiating topic is what we have called human closeness, and that closeness can exist in any type of relationship. It turns out that this topic (and not the sex scenes in the "Red Room of Pain") actually makes up 21 percent of

Fifty Shades of Grey. James was therefore writing in a different way from many other authors whose novels are labeled "erotica."

The second dominant topic in *Fifty Shades* is not BDSM either. It is something complementary to human closeness. This topic is about intimate conversation, which makes up another 13 percent of the novel, and reflects Ana's emotional discussions not just with Christian but with her best friend, Kate, her mother, her friend José, and her stepfather. A third important topic in James's novel, accounting for roughly 10 percent of the topical DNA, is one that centers on nonverbal communication such as smiles, glances, and other facial expressions. We learned that actually, when the novel is machine-read word for word, not one of the three most dominant topics in the novel is about kinky sex. To be sure, sex is there in the topical profile: the fourth, fifth, and sixth most prevalent topics taken together add another 13 percent of the overall ingredients and all of these relate to seduction, sex, and the female body. But clearly there was something else going on, something more subtle and more interesting than the BDSM hype that became the center of so much of the reviews. We saw this and realized the likely injustice in some review comments such as "This book is an example of how NOT to write a novel." It seemed that E. L. James might have actually mastered a few aspects of popular novel writing. In terms of thematics, she had got many things right in line with the market's taste. Two topics taking 30 percent of the novel? Check. A third topic taking us to 40 percent? Check. Closeness as one of those topics? Check. These are the tricks, conscious or unconscious, of hundreds of *NYT* bestselling authors, in all different genres. But we thought she might have other things to teach us.

The topic model alone showed us that it is not quite right to claim that the success of *Fifty Shades* was a lucky shot, a random occurrence in a crapshoot market. It also got us hooked on this book. James was being insulted all over the media and online forums—her book was trash, she didn't deserve her fame, she had no training, her novel was a fluke—and yet we were willing to tell ourselves that people don't suddenly make tens (or even hundreds) of millions of dollars by accident. They don't bring the world to its feet haphazardly. In any other field, that idea would be totally preposterous. We watched E. L. James change the world of publishing and reignite reading for millions of people, and thought perhaps she knew *just* what she was doing. The breakout success of her book surely could not *really* be an aberration, an error of literary history? We felt, having read it, that the book was in fact no black swan. We just had to demonstrate its latent secrets.

The topic model had given us a fragment, a hint. The critics' decision that "kinky fuckery" was the explanation for the sales numbers was likely a red herring. The novel is not so much outright erotica but is instead a spicy romance that has the emotional connection between its hero and heroine as its central interest. The sex in the novel is audacious, and it made for sensational headlines, but it's the constantly recurring question of whether or not Ana will submit or not—and all those fiery arguments between the lovers—that likely made this book more tantalizing than pure erotica.

The niggling problem with James's topical makeup on paper is that the top three topics don't immediately suggest conflict. Even without reading a new manuscript, our research has made us weary of overarching topics that unless handled wonderfully, won't give an author lots of space for interesting conflict to keep the plot turning. It is easy to see how Danielle Steel's use of human closeness as a first topic and hospitals as a second has the potential to get some pages turning. But E. L. James gives us first closeness and then intimate conversation. They look the same.

Conflict drives novels: like some critics and readers, we might look at these topics that make up 30 percent of *Fifty Shades of Grey* and wonder how the writer is going to achieve something gripping, either with plot or with character. Doesn't the presence in a love story of intimacy and closeness in high proportion suggest the happy ending rather than the three hundred pages of conflict that come before that moment of closure? Well, not for our hero Christian. Given the emotional background James paints for Christian, closeness and intimacy are his endless conflict and *are* his ongoing struggle. That twist shows the presence of the dark, Byronesque male love interest who has been popular with readers since Hardy and the Brontës. While the tortured masculine might be enough to start the pages turning, there is something else going on that makes them turn as quickly and as readily as they did for millions of readers. The thematic makeup for *Fifty Shades* just didn't *feel* quite right as the *full* explanation of why E. L. James belongs in a stable of mega-bestselling authors.

There are almost 509,000 5-star ratings of *Fifty Shades* on

Goodreads, and there is a trend to the 5-star reviews. P. A. Lupton wrote to other potential fans:

1. Please ensure that you have Kleenex prepared when you read this novel as build up of emotions will unavoidably lead to the inadvertent shedding of tears.

2. Make certain to schedule ample time for reading as once you begin you will be unable to put your book down.

3. IMPORTANT: Cold liquids, ice, cool cloths, or any cooling equipment such as central air or electric fans should be close at hand.

Another reader, Claire, wrote a direct address to the fictional Christian.

Sir. It seems that my every waking moment is about you. I have even dreamt about you. I have been so addicted to your story that I have grabbed every moment I could to read about you. I have skipped meals because that would take me away from you.

Two more capture the point. Juliana said:

I was on one of those this-romance-is-unbelievably-fantastic highs and the book had some surprisingly good humor. I had a pleasant feeling of anticipation as I read, but I was also extremely nervous.

James's fans are really showing us something here. In describing their reading experience, they endlessly reference the body. P. A. Lupton talks of shedding tears and overheating. Claire talks of ignoring the call to eat and sleep. Juliana talks of the bodily sensations of anticipation and nervousness. We absorbed what the Goodreaders were telling us and read the book again, with different kinds of attention. Then we hit upon it—our hypothesis on James. The closeness and intimacy topics are the foundations of the success of *Fifty Shades of Grey*, but they are not the skyscraper that was built upon them.

The Body Code

When we learned to read in high school, most of us were taught to read critically. We were taught to read with the mind, to analyze, discern, and find meaning. We have all had to write those essays at some point, and we find that many people who have continued to do that to make a living go with the same basic approach. English professors and essayists in the literary reviews tend to concentrate on forming interpretation and judgment based on the aspect of reading that is an experience of the rational mind. Take some of the dismissals of *Fifty Shades of Grey*. Critics and erotica writers have voiced some of the core complaints of the intellect. How could Anastasia have gotten through her BA degree without owning her own laptop? How likely is it that she really would have multiple orgasms during her first sexual experience? How could Christian, still in his twenties, conceivably be a self-made billionaire and beautifully handsome? How feasible is a commute between Portland and

Seattle? These supposed insults to rational common sense have been enough to render the book's success incomprehensible.

Other commentators found the *Fifty* phenomenon irritating based on their own analysis of the supposed *meaning* of the book. Apparently, Christian and Ana don't accurately represent a genuine BDSM community. Supposedly, Christian's story is too much like a weak pop psychology approach to abuse, sexual preference, and healing. We have also read the complaint many times that Ana's willingness to be a sexual submissive suggests that E. L. James herself is anti-feminist.

All these assertions (which indicate an understanding of novels that seems to ignore the fact that they are fiction and not critical essays) are based on giving primacy to the mind when we read—to hunting for an interpretation and some sort of easily canned "lesson" to take away.

That probably isn't the best way to approach a happy understanding of the success of this book. Needless to say, it's not really a "mind novel." *Fifty Shades of Grey,* more than many other books, is one of those that really demands we ask and be honest about the different reasons people read fiction. Its success, unless we are willing to just dismiss it, begs us to think deeply about the questions: What makes a book good? Who says so? And based on what criteria? We think answers to these kinds of questions might help address the confusion represented by the New Jersey bookseller who saw that her shoppers thought *Fifty Shades* was dumb and badly written but got totally addicted anyway. While the novel was never going to impress the Pulitzer Prize committee, the attention of more than 125 million people is worth thinking about. That attention shows, that like it or not, the novel *works* in ways that other novels just do not.

The rave reviews of *Fifty Shades of Grey* made a case for serious consideration of the emotional and visceral responses to literature. The readers kept repeating that the novel emotionally triggered them, viscerally triggered them, physically triggered them. They insisted that the pleasure of reading is not necessarily just about providing pleasure to the mind, but to the heart, the emotions, the body, and—for those who believe in these things—the soul. The problem is that this kind of appreciation of literature has been shrouded in embarrassment and shame for a long time. One literary agent gave a nice analogy to describe her enjoyment of *Fifty Shades*. She wrote: "I cringe the same way when I add an extra scoop of ice cream to my sundae or sneak chocolate while on a diet—because what I'm doing feels so good, it must mean trouble."* Guilty pleasures!

The history of this kind of shaming of what *feels* good when we read goes back a long way. From 1774 to 1820 only ninety fiction titles were published in the U.S., but by the 1840s this number was up to 800. The number was growing to meet demand, especially among female readers, who devoured novels and demanded more. Straightaway, the enjoyment of these novels was demeaned by most people with access to printed opinion. In 1855, the major runaway bestseller was a novel by Maria Susanna Cummins called *The Lamplighter*. The novel

---

* This and other comments on *Fifty Shades of Grey* are collected in *Fifty Writers on Fifty Shades of Grey*.

sold a huge number of copies for its time—70,000 in its first year and another 100,000 copies in Britain. It was widely read for many decades. One reviewer called it "one of the most original and natural narratives," but Nathaniel Hawthorne— who as a prominent literary writer of his time had an influential vote that often still holds—disliked it. Hawthorne asked his editor, "What is the mystery of these innumerable editions of *The Lamplighter?*" Like many reviewers then and since, he was perplexed by bestselling and couldn't explain it. He told his editor that he would rather give up writing than be associated with "this damned mob of scribbling women," who wrote the "trash" with which America was preoccupied. It's a sentiment that has stuck.

The Lamplighter is about a young, unloved orphan girl, Gerty, who is rescued from an abusive guardian and taught love, good moral values, and faith while retaining a touch of wildness and backbone. Of course, by the end of the book she has gone through a lot of growth, and she finally wins her man. Despite its huge fan base, Hawthorne considered the novel too sentimental.

The following century James Joyce introduced us to Gerty McDowell in *Ulysses*. Joyce's Gerty is an unflattering parody of *The Lamplighter*'s heroine: she is "flawed" with a crippled foot, full of impure thoughts, and her chief concern is her "undies." Neither canonical male writer was willing to take Cummins's Gerty or her story seriously despite the novel's mass success. Both objected to (and shamed) the novel for its reliance on strong emotional response.

One hundred fifty years later, the reviewing community

book, you can make an instinctive guess about which one belongs to the book that captured the mainstream market. The
difference between breakout affective DNA and lower-selling
DNA is laid bare. These three novels share some of the same
themes—billionaires, love, sex, troubled personalities—but
topical makeup alone does not make a global bestseller. *Addicted to You* is a heavier book emotionally—both characters
are addicts and both have to hit rock bottom. For that reason,
the emotional line stays below zero for much of the book. *Playing Games* is clearly lighter.

Changes in direction on the graphs roughly equate to
moments of conflict and resolution. The more frequent the
peaks and valleys are, the more of an emotional roller coaster
for the characters and for readers. The gradient of the peaks
and valleys shows the intensity of changes in emotion. All
this stuff translates in the market and in book reviews into
words like "page-turner," "suspenseful," "gripping," and "addictive."

We have a personal friend whose agent could not sell his
latest novel: seven major editors said they really liked it, but
something was off for them, something made them feel they
had to pass. This something can be described as that certain *je
ne sais quoi,* a textual charisma or magnetism that gives it the
same sort of sparkle that belongs to those people who can walk
into any room and stop it dead. Computer reading makes that
magnetism a little easier to understand.

We processed our friend's novel, showed him the emotional
arc, and he learned something immediately. The graph showed
him that he had not yet succeeded with one of the best pieces

of advice given to writers who want to sell, a rule that John Grisham swears by. That rule is that you must hook your reader within the first forty pages, which most acquisitions editors would find rather generous. That's all the time you have to capture your reader by her gut or her heart or the back of her neck.

And the difference between a soft emotional response like a chuckle or an inward smile and the sort of response that grabs your readers by the scruff of their neck is represented pictorially in the sharpness of the first peak or valley on a graph. That's your hook. If it's not there, you have likely written one of those books that people give up on after a couple of chapters. Sorry. Conversely, if there's a book on your nightstand that you tell yourself you "really should read" but you can't seem to manage more than two paragraphs at bedtime, then the curves are likely to be all wrong for a blockbuster hit.

Our friend had his peaks and valleys, and the two erotic romance novels we've shown that were not by E. L. James have them, too, but his first one was more of a bump than a mountain. His emotional opening was there, and that got him into the hands of seven editors, but it was a whispering beckon and not a steel fishhook. He rewrote his opening with more emotion and drama. He raised the stakes for his characters, increased their conflict. His curves grew and balanced, and editors bit.

Let's have another look at E. L. James's perfect curves. Almost symmetrical, perfectly rhythmic, and with an amplitude and frequency to keep conflict high and readers on the edge of

Major Scenes in Fifty Shades of Grey

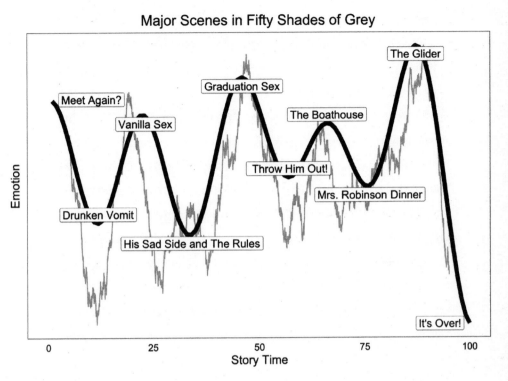

Fig. 5.

their seats. Here is the book with some key scenes shown in Figure 5.

The lighter, more frenetic line behind the black one shows the higher-frequency heartbeat of the novel, and readers who have read *Fifty Shades* ten times (and we are told there are many), will likely be able to recognize every little change in emotional direction. All those scratchy ups and downs reflect the excitement and pain in Ana's heart as she and Christian understand and misunderstand each other, which happens more or less every few pages. This constant micro-level conflict and resolution translates as the chemistry between the lovers—the major ongoing hook of the book—and when is chemistry ever a straight, flat line?

In computer modeling, though, we can smooth the curve to highlight the lower frequency pulse of emotion. This black line tells the story of the book and to some extent the pace of its plotting. If you have never read *Fifty Shades,* reading these labeled scenes and the curves they sit on will give you the book in about sixty seconds. The downward slope of the first valley begins when Ana has been sent to interview Christian in his office and finds that one of the scripted questions she has to ask him is if he is gay. Given the spark between them, the intrusive nature of the question, and the unlikeliness that Christian is gay (there is already palpable heat between them!), the question embarrasses Ana. How this moment makes Ana wince! She manages, however, to make a much bigger fool of herself some pages later. Look at the bottom of the first valley on the graph. During that scene, Ana, who cannot handle her alcohol, gets drunk in a bar and starts feeling brave. She makes one of those phone calls that many of us have made and regretted. When Christian turns up at the bar in response to her hanging up on him, she notes how gorgeous he is before vomiting all over the azaleas.

Not cool.

The peak on the graph labeled "vanilla sex" is where, having confessed her virginity and her desire to lose it, Ana succumbs to Christian and spends several pages having many ecstatic orgasms. The novel continues like this—up and down—until the highest point toward the end. In the glider scene, in which Christian surprises Ana with a thrilling day cartwheeling in the sky, the couple feel their most joyful and free. It's a rare occasion when Christian's mood is not hooded and Ana is not overthinking everything.

Typically a big high point like this would signal the approach of a happy ending, as we expect with a romance novel. But anyone who has read *Fifty Shades* knows that E. L. James defied that implicit contract at the last minute, and instead of marrying the lovers, she splits them up. What defiance on James's part! Look how quickly and steeply the plotted line drops—we can feel from it the fast breaking of both hearts when Ana pushes Christian too far in the playroom, regrets it, and flees him forever. The book ends with despair for both characters and for any reader who has been emotionally engaged. We want a different ending!

It's no surprise, then, that book two sold as well as it did.

If we smooth the *Fifty Shades* curve a little more, we can see more evidence of practiced plotting. Teachers of any narrative art, be it novels, movies, or plays, talk about a three-act structure, and have done so since the ancient Greeks. This is sometimes called setup, confrontation, and resolution, or a bit less formally, rising action, climax, and falling action. A writer who has internalized this basic structure will be aware of the need for a plot turn at about one-third of the way through her novel and then again at about two-thirds. When we zoom to this level, we see *Fifty Shades* from a less granular perspective, but we can still get from it the basic shape of the plot, which at this

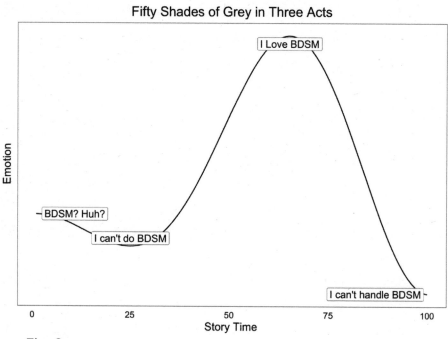

Fig. 6.

macro-level shows that the book is not so much "all about BDSM" but about Ana's changing opinion about it. See Figure 6.

When we plotted all of the books in our entire corpus on this same scale, we found that novels can be divided into seven different fundamental plot shapes. Some specific examples of each of these shapes might show slight variations—perhaps the first curve, for example, is a little more exaggerated in one novel than the next, or perhaps the ending is more sharply positive in one of the novels than another. But the stories collected together under each of the seven plotlines will follow the basic trajectory, and all the novels in our entire research collection fit one of the seven.

Plotline 1

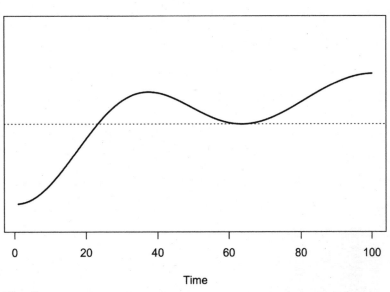

Fig. 7.

The simplest way to comprehend the seven plotlines (shown here in Figures 7–13) is to note the three-act structure, the midpoint, and the difference between the beginning and the end. Note, then, what happens at about 30–35 percent, at 60–65 percent, and at 50 percent. These are the typical moments in novels for changes in the fortunes of the protagonist. Note also whether the story ends in happier or less fortunate emotional terrain.

Plot 1 (Fig. 7) is a story about the gradual move from difficult times to happy times. The features of this story are an ending that is happier than the starting place, an opening in some sort of difficulty, and some scenes, just when things are looking up, that threaten the happy change. While we have bestselling examples in our corpus of all seven plotlines, there is

Plotline 2

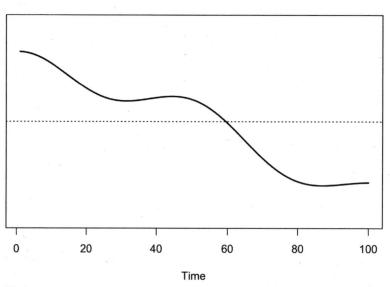

Time

Fig. 8.

no outright sure bet here for writing a bestselling manuscript. Some of the novels the model assigned to this one include John Grisham's *The Client*, Kim Edwards's *The Memory Keeper's Daughter*, James Patterson's *I, Alex Cross*, Nora Roberts *Morrigan's Cross*, and Sue Monk Kidd's *The Invention of Wings* and *The Secret Life of Bees*.

Plot 2 (Fig. 8) appears to be the inverse of Plot 1. Examples of this kind of general plotline are *The Devil Wears Prada* by Lauren Weisberger, *Notorious Nineteen* by Janet Evanovich, *The Bonfire of the Vanities* by Tom Wolfe, *Rainbow Six* by Tom Clancy, and *All the Light We Cannot See* by Anthony Doer. In different versions of this type of story, the plotline may be more or less straight. Perhaps the temporary upward lift round about the middle is stronger and more hopeful in some novels than others. But this story has a character in a difficult world who is likely also making some misguided decisions. Perhaps the plot shows a slight lift at the end—note how the archetypal line is quite flat for the last fifth of the book rather than dipping deeper and deeper into tragedy right up to the last page. This part of the story might, then, show a character coming to terms with the real low point at about 80 percent of the way through.

We are aware, of course, that we are not the first literary critics to have suggested there are a finite number of literary plots, although Matt was likely the first to suggest it with computational evidence.* In 1959, William Foster-Harris claimed there are three: the happy ending, the unhappy ending, and the literary plot. In 1993, Ronald Tobias suggested twenty. There have also been cases made for just one universal plot, and for as many as thirty-six. The critic most known for claiming there are seven is Christopher Booker, who spent decades reading thousands of stories in order to support his hypothesis.

As we studied the plotlines the computer gave us, and looked back at Booker's work, we found some compelling crossover. While Booker is a Jungian scholar who shows no graphic representation of plot shape, and we are working here with code based on different valences of positive and negative words, we believe our findings are supportive of Booker's basic prem-

---

* Matt's work on plot received some media attention in 2014. Since then he has completely rewritten and validated the algorithms. The work presented here is entirely new and based on a different collection of books.

ise, and that his explanations of seven plots roughly map onto the shapes we have found.

Plots 1 and 2 might be close to what Booker calls Comedy and Tragedy. Comedy in literary criticism is not so much about a story that makes us laugh, but rather one in which a central character or characters gradually overcome a sometimes absurd and complex set of problems in order to find a happy ending. The plotline has been labeled "from confusion to enlightenment," and tends to feature miscommunications, separations, and other hiccups that mean final happiness takes 300 and not 30 pages. This theory does seem to fit the first of our plot shapes, just as its inverse, Plot 2, looks like the plot that Booker and others have called Tragedy. Again, a tragic plot may not necessarily indicate hell for everyone. *The Devil Wears Prada* is not *Hamlet*. But Weisberger's protagonist Andrea learns some fairly tough lessons, and many of these lessons come because she is ignoring the sound wisdom of her own intuition and the people who love her. Pride, or *hubris,* is a commonly named flaw in tragic theory, and it tends to propel a character's journey into pretty murky emotional terrain. This kind of plot is often about the internal conflicts and flaws of the lead character, and how that character falls victim to those flaws, as much as it might be about the "evil" of a secondary character and worldly circumstances that also make their life difficult. The novels in this group tend to end with some sadness because while the protagonists might realize the error of their ways, it might be too late. Andrea, for example, loses her boyfriend and threatens her

Plotline 3

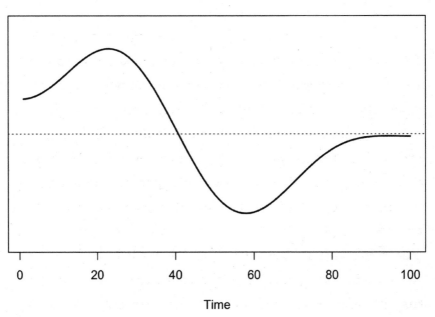

Time

Fig. 9.

relationships with her family for the sake of her controlling boss and a job at *Runway Magazine*. By the time she realizes the mistake and quits, she can only move back in with her parents and try to start again in a different part of the magazine industry.

Plot 3 (Fig. 9) might be called the Coming-of-Age story or the Rags-to-Riches plot (which is what Booker calls it), and certainly this is where *Cinderella* and *Jane Eyre* belong. But the label shouldn't imply there is always a young protagonist present: rather it simply suggests that there is some central movement between success and crisis.

The important plotting element of this shape is that first a

Plotline 4

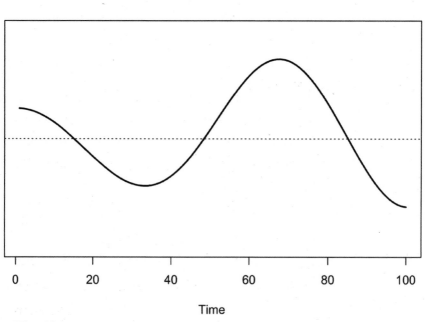

Time

Fig. 10.

main character experiences a happy turn of fate (e.g., Cinderella meets Prince Charming at a ball), and then loses everything (the clock strikes midnight), before returning from despair to some kind of fulfillment or peaceful closure. This plot need not suggest a love story: indeed there are novels of all genres in all these groups. Some of the bestsellers in this group include Anita Shreve's *Testimony,* Amy Tan's *The Kitchen God's Wife,* Stephen King's *Misery,* Robert Ludlum's *The Aquitaine Progression,* and Liane Moriarty's *Big Little Lies.*

Plot 4 (Fig. 10), the inverse of 3, is where *Fifty Shades of Grey* belongs. This is likely the plotline that Booker called Rebirth because for him these plots tend to see the main characters experience change, renewal, and some sort of transformation. Often there is a strong influence, typically dark or corruptive, and therefore the first act shows a dip in emotional terrain as the protagonist's values are tested and their world becomes more complex. In this first dip the character may experience something like a crisis in confidence or low self-esteem before rising to new learning, new experience, and new expressions of themself. The typically negative ending might show a lack of closure or a crisis as the character struggles with a change brought on by someone else.

Hilary Mantel's novel *Wolf Hall,* which won the Booker Prize, is another example of this kind of plot. The novel tells Mantel's interpretation of Thomas Cromwell's story in the court of Henry VIII, covering the tumultuous period when the king wanted to get divorced from Catherine of Aragon in order to marry Anne Boleyn. There are potentially sinister threats all around Cromwell, and his story is one of perseverance. At the end of this novel about the total transformation of church and state in England, Cardinal Wolsey dies and Anne has failed to produce a male heir. All is not yet well.

Other novels with this plot shape include Paula McLain's *The Paris Wife,* Stephen King's *The Stand,* Jodi Picoult's *Leaving Time,* and Kate Morton's *The Forgotten Garden.*

Plots 5 and 6 (Figs. 11, 12), also the mirrors of one another, share a pivot around the 50 percent mark, and therefore have the double dip of the W shape or the double peak of the M. Plot 5, which includes novels such as Nicholas Sparks's *The Notebook* and *The Last Song,* Cormac McCarthy's *The Road,* James Patterson's *Hope to Die,* and Irene Nemirovsky's *Suite*

Plotline 5

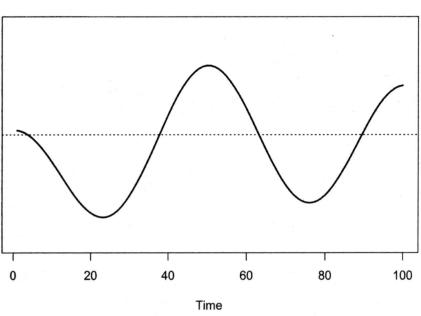

Fig. 11.

Française, is close to what Booker calls the Voyage and Return plot. For Booker, these stories are about characters who are confronted with or plunged into a whole other world, find some fascination with it, experience a dark turn, and then end with a happy return to some sort of normalcy. Booker cites many stories in which the character takes a physical journey into an odd new world—*Alice in Wonderland* and *Gulliver's Travels* are classic examples—but the journey might also be emotional or intellectual. The lover protagonists of *The Notebook* both confront the new worlds of each other's backgrounds, one wealthy, the other poor, as well as the new terrain they must

Plotline 6

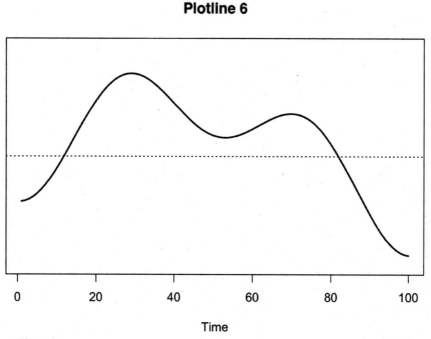

Fig. 12.

cover when Allie suffers dementia and forgets most of their life story. Plot 5 is chosen by many romance novelists, who have the high point of the first love scene at the halfway point and then introduce a plot twist to part the lovers before they reunite at the end.

Plot 6 (Fig. 12) is the story of the Quest. This is about seeking and finding, it's about unknown territories, fighting monsters—literal and metaphorical—experiencing unexpected adventures, dashed hopes, and, finally, a quest in some way completed. Some of the novels the model assigned to this group were Jonathan Franzen's *The Corrections*, Salman Rushdie's *The Satanic Verses*, Kristin Hannah's *Firefly Lane*, Mitch

Plotline 7

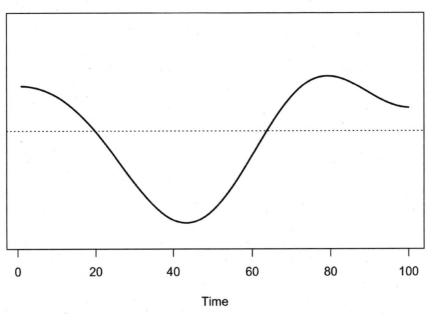

Time

Fig. 13.

Albom's *The First Phone Call from Heaven,* and Emily Giffin's *Love the One You're With.*

The final plotline, Plot 7 (Fig. 13), has no inverse. Kurt Vonnegut has called this the "man in hole story"*; Booker calls it Overcoming the Monster. It is often about a hero and a bad guy where there is some threat to a person or a culture that must be eliminated. The threat might be a dragon or a disease, a situation or a system, but the main character is forced to take it on and then change his or her fortunes back to good.

---

* His short video on the shapes of stories is well worth the watch, and is available on YouTube: https://www.youtube.com/watch?v=oP3c1h8v2ZQ.

Novels with this plotline include Chris Cleave's *Little Bee*, Anita Diamant's *The Boston Girl*, John Grisham's *The Runaway Journey*, Matthew Quick's *The Silver Linings Playbook*, and Charlaine Harris's *From Dead to Worse*.

Given the other plotlines had come in pairs, we thought about the inverse of Plot 7, a potential Plot 8, in which things go from quite bad to really good then to quite bad again. The computer never drew this shape—the man on mountain to go with the man in hole. No bestseller in any genre that we could find has such a plotline. But we decided it makes perfect sense: Who would want to read such a story?

While it is true that there are some bestsellers in all seven groups of plots, we found that in the whole collection of books we were working with, only a small number had a shape that closely matched the shape seen in *Fifty Shades*. A list of the twenty-five most similar books is at the end of this chapter but consider the names and careers of a few of the authors who make the list: Stephen King, Jackie Collins, Dan Brown, Sylvia Day, Danielle Steel, Lee Child, James Patterson. All of these are million-copy writers.

Lone Stars

The two books for adults over the past couple of decades that have been insanely successful (and by "books for adults" we really mean books that are not *Harry Potter*), are *Fifty Shades of Grey* and Dan Brown's *The Da Vinci Code*. While *Inferno* is the only Dan Brown novel among those twenty-five novels with a

The Da Vinci Code and Fifty Shades of Grey

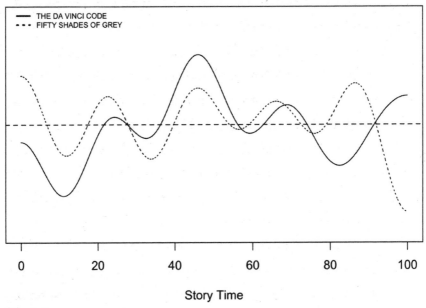

Fig. 14.

the three-act plot movement similar to *Fifty Shades*, *The Da Vinci Code* is the only novel in our collection of bestsellers that closely shares the regular rhythmic beat of *Fifty Shades*. When looked at together, these graphs create a very powerful image. It seems there could be some sort of patterning to counter the popular claim that their stratospheric success was totally random.

With the exception of the endings, look at how well these two plotlines mirror each other (Fig. 14), in two ostensibly different books. It would be easy to think that the novels have nothing in common. They have totally different authors, different genres, different themes, different styles. But both authors have mastered a way of tapping into a reader's heart and gut like few others have. Across our entire corpus there are a handful of books that exhibit this regularity of emotional beat, but *Fifty Shades* and *Da Vinci Code* are two of the most regular in our entire collection. The distance between each peak is about the same, and the distance between each valley is about the same, and finally, the distances between peaks and valleys are about the same. This reflects a deep attunement to the kind of pacing that the market—and let's be honest, it's a global market for those books—seems to most enjoy. In other words, both novels have mastered the page-turner beat. There is a symmetry to these books that is very unusual, and they really differ only because *Fifty Shades*, being the first book in a series rather than a stand-alone story, gives us the low-point ending to anticipate book two. In both novels, the characters' actions at the high and low points are almost always physical, visceral, and totally embodied. Characters are panting; readers are panting. In James the regular high beats are about sex; in Brown the high points are moments of relief between low points of being chased and on the run (see Fig. 15).

Do these graphs represent a glorious accident or careful, strategic plotting? Only the authors themselves know the answer to that. But the graphs seem to solve a major literary riddle. We know we'd invest in a manuscript if we saw that graph appear again!

So how do we do this? How do we take something as intangible as emotional and visceral response and render it in

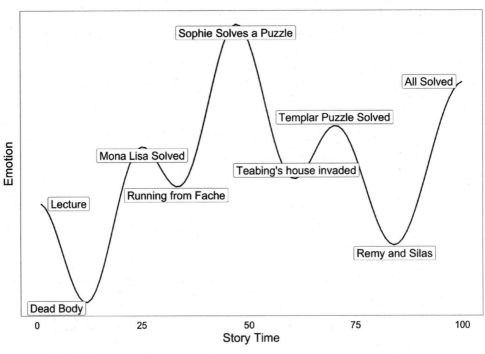

Fig. 15.

black ink on the page? Displaying the ups and downs of emotion as curves is facilitated by what researchers in natural language processing call sentiment analysis. Work in this field has included the computational study of online movie and product reviews, but we've found that the same tools and techniques can be applied to the study of narrative. The basic idea is that you train a computer to read through a book from beginning to end while paying special attention to positive and negative emotional language. Consider this simple scene from *The Da Vinci Code*. Sophie is fondly recalling "her first code" and the "encoded archway" that her grandfather took her to at Rosslyn Chapel as a child:

He led her over to the elaborate archway he had shown her earlier. Sophie immediately plopped down on the stone floor, lying on her back and staring up at the collage of puzzle pieces overhead. "I'm going to break this code before you get back!"

"It's a race then." He bent over, kissed her forehead, and walked to the nearby side door.

This is one of many similar interludes in an otherwise frenetic narrative in which Brown pauses the action and provides backstory. Our machine recognizes this as a moment of lightness, a positive pause in an action-packed narrative. The sentiment is positive; the scene shows us something personal, soft, and reflective in an otherwise high action, high stress story. We can feel the fondness in the scene.

Contrast this scene of Sophie's childhood of relative calm and peace with Silas's recollections of his own past:

Still, the memories haunted his soul. Release your hatred, Silas commanded himself. Forgive those who trespassed against you. Looking up at the stone towers of Saint-Sulpice, Silas fought that familiar undertow . . . that force that often dragged his mind back in time, locking him once again in the prison that had been his world as a young man. The memories of purgatory came as they always did, like a tempest to his senses . . . the reek of rotting cabbage, the stench of death, human urine and feces. The cries of hopelessness against the howling wind of the Pyrenees and the soft sobs of forgotten men.

The emotional difference between the two flashbacks is obvious, and it is also obvious to the machine.

Over the course of a narrative, these moments of positive and negative emotion accumulate and dissipate in interesting and dynamic ways. Each novel has its own unique journey as the author moves us through whichever periods of conflict and conflict resolution they write to keep the characters moving through time. At the macroscale, these accumulated moments become like marks of punctuation in the narrative arc of the novel, and the highs and lows of feeling that the machine detects mark the most important and pivotal points of the story. From this data, the machine can draw the graphs for every novel with more or less granularity.

In the end, hundreds of plotlines showed us that bestsellers can have any of the fundamental three-part plot shapes. A "man in hole" story doesn't necessarily have more of a chance in the market than a "rags to riches" plot. And though the macroshape doesn't particularly matter, how the author works the scene-by-scene rhythm into that shape is very important. The million-dollar move is in a good, strong, regular beat.

The Lists: Plot

Top ten with a macroshape like *Fifty Shades of Grey*

1. Dan Brown, *Inferno*
2. Lee Child, *Killing Floor*
3. Jackie Collins, *Lucky*

4. Michael Connelly, *The Burning Room*
5. Sylvia Day, *Entwined with You*
6. Dave Eggers, *The Circle*
7. Robert Galbraith, *The Cuckoo's Calling*
8. Chad Harbach, *The Art of Fielding*
9. Stephen King, *Cujo*
10. Jodi Picoult, *Leaving Time*

Top ten with a rhythmic beat (excluding *Fifty Shades of Grey* and *The Da Vinci Code*)

1. Tom Clancy, *Patriot Games*
2. Tom Clancy, *The Teeth of the Tiger*
3. Graeme Simsion, *The Rosie Project*
4. Judith Krantz, *I'll Take Manhattan*
5. George R. R. Martin, *A Game of Thrones*
6. James Patterson, *Alex Cross, Run*
7. James Patterson, *Sundays at Tiffany's*
8. Martin Cruz Smith, *Polar Star*
9. Nicholas Sparks, *Dear John*
10. Tom Wolfe, *The Bonfire of the Vanities*

4

THE **DEBUTANTES,** OR, **WHY EVERY COMMA MATTERS**

In early July of 2013 a U.S. professor received a random phone call from across the Atlantic. The stranger on the end of the line asked him to help solve a mystery. The professor was asked to bring his special expertise in hidden patterns to correct history. Within a week he would be in the spotlight, all over the international news.

The story sounds just like something Dan Brown would make up and then sell about a hundred million copies. But in this instance, the professor was not Robert Langdon but Patrick Juola, his domain was not symbology but stylometrics, and his case study was not the Catholic Church but J. K. Rowling. Juola, a professor of computer science and an expert on computational authorship attribution, was asked by a *Sunday Times* news reporter to investigate a new novel. That novel was *The Cuckoo's Calling* by Robert Galbraith, a debut author who had ostensibly drawn on his years as a member of the Royal Military

Police to write a detective story. But the reporter had been tipped off. The anonymous hint was that Galbraith didn't really exist and that the real author was in fact the *Harry Potter* creator. Was it true? Juola worked on the case. Within thirty minutes, his computer gave him sufficient evidence to support the tip-off. Could he *prove* Rowling authored the book? No. But he would have bet on it. On July 13, J. K. Rowling reluctantly, but publicly, confessed that she was indeed the author.

Rowling claimed that she had written under the name Robert Galbraith because a clean name would enable her to receive feedback without expectations. It's not easy, if you happen to be that person who created and sold 500 million copies of *Harry Potter,* to do much without fanfare and scrutiny. Could she ever get a viewpoint on her work as a novelist without the filter of her fame?

Probably not. Not unless she used a pseudonym. But as Rowling found out, creating a new name when your work is already out there is not so easy to do. She changed her genre, her audience, her topics, and her plotline. She claimed her intention was to "successfully channel her inner bloke," to write, as it were, "like a man," called Robert. In writing for adults and not children, she also consciously chose a different level of vocabulary. But as Rowling would learn, it is very difficult to change or hide one's linguistic fingerprint.

Think of it this way. Jodie is fair, blue eyed, and five feet four inches tall. None of this is what she would call her style. It's a manifestation of her foundational DNA. She can do what she can to try to change these manifestations. She can wear colored lenses, she can dye her hair jet-black, and she can wear high heels or a man's clothes. But without genetic engineering, her DNA will keep repeating the same patterns as her cells renew. She can wear a business suit or a party dress to change the impression. She can change her style, if she wants, every season. But what she can't alter all that much is what Nature has given her to work with. Her foundation—her bone structure—isn't going to change. And one strand of her hair, blond or black, will tell anyone with the right microscope who she is.

It's strange—mind-blowing even—to think that a person's writing might contain something like this foundational DNA. While it is true the unique way that an author uses words is not quite the same as that author's individual and biological gene expressions, years of research in authorship attribution and stylometrics have suggested that each of us has a fairly unique and individual linguistic fingerprint or style. Even when Rowling tried, very consciously, to write like "Robert Galbraith" and not like J. K. Rowling, there were habits and patterns to her prose that she could not successfully suppress. It took Juola's computer only a matter of minutes to detect and identify these patterns, and these were all about aspects of narrative we often overlook—things like the use of prepositions, pronouns, and grammatical marks.

Naturally, some writers are more similar to each other than others just as some people look more alike than others. In some situations, when there are expected conventions, many different writers may make very similar choices. A business letter might be one example. Similarly, there are a number of external factors that will impact how a sole writer writes—intended purpose and audience being the major ones. Just consider the mortifying embarrassment that comes with clicking "send" on an email that has been mistakenly addressed to the wrong person! We tend not to write to our boss in the same way we might write to our best friend, even if the topic in both potential emails is our opinion on whether we deserve a raise. So it is not always a simple matter to distinguish between two different writers, or even the same writer in different circumstances. Nevertheless, at some level, all of us have unconscious habits of style. Whether we think deeply about every adjective choice and comma we use or whether we sit and write in a flurry, we all have linguistic tics that subtly mark our personal style. Because they are hidden from the naked eye, but are nonetheless detectable to an algorithm, it's convenient to call these individual writing tics a kind of linguistic DNA. Admittedly, genetic and linguistic DNA are not quite the same thing, but there are some very interesting comparisons to be made. Matt's research with Daniela Witten has even shown that some machine-learning methods developed specifically for the analysis of genetic DNA are equally effective when analyzing linguistic data.[*]

In the very simplest sense, genes determine how a cell functions. Scientists and statisticians working in the field of bioinformatics will sometimes analyze gene expression data as a way of predicting different types of biological outcomes. It turns out, for example, that the extent to which certain genes are expressed or not can be a telling indicator of cancer. If we think about words as being similar to genes, then we can say

---

[*] Their study, "A Comparative Study of Machine Learning Methods for Authorship Attribution," is found in *Literary and Linguistic Computing*, 25.2, 2010, 215–224.

that these word-genes determine how a book functions. As we saw in chapter 2, some words are the building blocks of theme. Nouns, in particular, can tell much about what a novel is about. But a novel is much more than just what it is about, and determining a bestseller or not involves looking at much more than just its topical makeup.

Stephen King's book *On Writing* reflects some deep thinking about the style of different authors and how their style is made. When it comes to writing well, King recommends that writers have a toolbox, which is full of the vocabulary that is natural to them. He also suggests using correct grammar and having an understanding of how things such as paragraph length contribute to the tone and pace of a story. A pacy, scary novel will tend to have shorter, punchier paragraphs. And so on. Given his meditations on style, you'd think that King could reinvent himself persuasively. But when he tried, he was outed too.

In the late 1970s, King decided to conceal his identity with the pen name Richard Bachman. He was interested in what he called a "talent vs. luck" debate, and he claims, as Rowling did, that he wanted to see what would happen to his new work without the impact of his established brand name. In King's case, it didn't even take a computer model to note the similarities in style. He was outed by a bookseller. As Bachman, King had written a novel called *Thinner,* which, ironically, was reviewed as "what Stephen King would write if Stephen King *could* write."*

---

* See James Smythe's article in the April 16, 2013, issue of *The Guardian.*

The first Bachman novels had not sold all that well, but this one was selling respectably. A bookseller in D.C. read it and thought that if this book was not by King, it was the best copycat of King's style he had ever seen. He wrote to King's publisher and King decided to confess to him in an interview.

Of course, as soon as news broke that Bachman was King, sales of *Thinner* went from 40,000 copies to 400,000, and his novel rocketed to number one. Robert Galbraith also shot up the charts when it was revealed that "he" was J. K. Rowling. But it's also true that both authors sold again as "debutantes" under pen names, and both were considered more accomplished in their genres than most debut writers. Given the thousands of horror, thriller, and crime writers competing in the market, how could two unknowns, Bachman and Galbraith, still manage to find so many readers? And for that matter, how do any first-time writers get noticed at all? One answer, as we'll see, lies in having a winning style.

What is fascinating to us is that this isn't so much about what a *New Yorker* reviewer might quote to illustrate a winning style—beautiful metaphor perhaps, or an ability to find the perfect words and expression for those complex sentiments most of us can only feel. Those reviewers occupy an important space in the literary world, and stylometrics, rather than seeking to do that same work, seeks to complement it in compelling ways. What we are looking at with the algorithms we use on style is not that perfectly ironic expression we love in good writing, or that stark but pleasurable shock of seeing the same old thing described in a simple new way. Instead, it is the most common and seemingly boring features of an author's prose, which ironically enough will tell you with much more statistical accuracy about which writers will sell and which ones will not than any fine appreciation of their unique metaphors.

It turns out that the frequency with which King uses the word "the" (for example, 4.8 percent in *Mr. Mercedes*) and Rowling uses the word "of" (2.1 percent in *The Cuckoo's Calling*) are telling indicators of market success. While these authors have of course already made it big—meaning you might fairly say, "Okay, King gets 'the' right but have you seen his marketing budget?"—this matter of the right basic words and marks of grammar in the right proportions can also determine whether someone's first novel has a realistic shot at being number one.

In short, style is important; it is the mechanism through which plot, theme, and character get delivered. Style is at once mechanical and organic; it springs from a combination of nature and nurture; from innate ability and practiced craft. And nowhere is the importance of style seen more vividly than in the work of those authors who are hitting the *NYT* list for the first time. Saying it is difficult to make it straight onto the *NYT* list with a first novel is a great understatement. The market is crowded with hundreds of thousands of books: thrillers, romances, crime novels, family sagas, and literary novels. When it comes to theme and plot, many of them can begin to look very much alike. As Booker Prize–finalist Chigozie Obioma noted in a recent BBC interview, there are no new stories, no new plots; there are only new ways of telling stories. What Obioma is talking about here is style. Style matters. Style is what helps a new writer appear new and engaging to his readers and not old hat or predictable. And when we cranked up our computers and programmed them to analyze the style of thousands of recent books, we found that to algorithms looking at likely success, style is *exactly* what refreshes a familiar tale.

Buy the Flowers

The computational study of authorial style we have been discussing is a branch of applied linguistics sometimes called stylometrics. In literary criticism these methods have been used to add evidence to the question of who authored canonical medieval texts such as *Sir Gawain and the Green Knight* and to explore questions about whether or not Shakespeare was the real author of the plays that carry his name. But the application of these methods goes beyond literary study. In one legal case, these methods of textual analysis were used to help provide political asylum for a refugee and in another case as evidence of plagiarism. So important are the legal and criminal applications, that an entire subbranch of the field has developed into what is called forensic linguistics, and experts have analyzed everything from the Unabomber manifesto to the JonBenet Ramsey ransom note. Who wrote what can have life-changing consequences.*

---

* One of the best-known cases of authorship attribution involves the Federalist Papers that were anonymously written by Alexander Hamilton, James Madison, and John Jay. As early as 1997, Richard S. Forsyth noted that the Federalist Papers problem "is possibly the best candidate for an accepted benchmark in stylometry." Matt and coauthor Daniela Witten analyzed the Federalist Papers in their aforementioned paper "A Comparative Study of Machine Learning Methods for Authorship Attribution." Matt's *Text Analysis with R for Students of Literature* includes several chapters devoted to authorship attribution and stylo-

In the world of fiction publishing, especially as a new writer, it's not so much who wrote what but how it was written that might change your life. Unlike literary topics, novelistic style is difficult to grasp without some concrete examples. We believe that the first line of a novel can tell you a lot about a writer's command of style. Here are three pretty famous opening ones:

Virginia Woolf opens *Mrs. Dalloway* elegantly: "Mrs. Dalloway said she would buy the flowers herself."

Leo Tolstoy starts *Anna Karenina* astutely: "Happy families are all alike; every unhappy family is unhappy in its own way."

Jane Austen starts *Pride and Prejudice* archly: "It is a truth universally acknowledged, that a single man in possession of a good fortune must be in want of a wife."

These sentences are quoted so often—praised and loved and almost fetishized—that any reader or writer of fiction might want to think about them. Why do they *work*? One thing that is immediately clear about all three of these classic writers is that their first sentences create voice. Note everything about them—the length, the punctuation, the relative simplicity. *Someone* is talking to us, and that someone sounds authentic, in command of some sort of authority. There is no wavering, or cautiousness, or lack of surety. All novelists have the challenge of creating some sort of selfhood, and readers might note that they tend to keep reading when that selfhood, attractive or not, at least knows itself and leads its reader. The best writers—or

---

metric analysis, and his chapter titled "Style" in *Macroanalysis: Digital Methods and Literary History* deals with many of the same methods.

those who will achieve the most readers—are able to establish this kind of presence from the opening sentence with tiny and seemingly effortless modulations in style.

It's not often that Jane Austen and Jackie Collins belong in the same sentence. It's not often that Stephen King is written about alongside Leo Tolstoy. But they are some of the most read writers out there, and there are reasons they should be talked about together. Here's the opening line of Jackie Collins's novel *Poor Little Bitch Girl*:

> Belle Svetlana surveyed her nude image in a full-length mirror, readying herself for a thirty-thousand-dollar-an-hour sexual encounter with the fifteen-year-old son of an Arab oil tycoon.

And here's a shorter one from King, from his contemporary classic *The Shining*:

"Jack Torrance thought: *Officious little prick.*"

To many critics, the perceived difference between the writers of these sentences and the classic writers is the difference between "highbrow" and "lowbrow," which for many roughly translates as "writers worth teaching in colleges" and "trash." It has been that way since the concept of a bestseller was first introduced. But why the snobbery? What, exactly, is the difference? Look at the first sentences again. Why should the classic writers be lauded as doing anything better than two of those writers in our contemporary culture who have *seriously* made it? Can't success just be success?

Look at the Austen next to the Collins again. There are similarities. Both openings show a woman in an arguably passive predicament in the hands of male patriarchy. Both voices—with some self-aware irony—introduce us to a fictional world in which the female characters will exchange sex and some "ownership" of themselves for the security of money that a man can provide. Even in Austen's world, we see some women paired off with men who likely are as unattractive to them as this "fifteen-year-old son of an Arab oil tycoon" is to Belle Svetlana. In Austen, the subordination of the female is done grammatically: the man *is in want of* a *wife*. The implied woman is relegated to the end of the sentence, described only in terms of her relationship to the man—as *wife*. *She* is, according to the structure of this sentence, to be a result of his "good fortune." The enduring voice of Austen's sentence is achieved through the wry distaste heard in the hyperbolic phrase "truth universally acknowledged." Which great novelist who understands the infinite subtleties of the human condition *really* talks, especially in the opening phrase of their masterwork, of *universal truths*? Two huge, loaded words. We are meant to see that the narrator is smirking at the whole situation. And thus Austen achieves brilliance. She achieves it without excessive clauses, without long-winded syntax, without the endless sentences of some classic writers who will write for three paragraphs without a period point. There is no need to write any sentence that would cause someone reading it aloud to need paramedics with oxygen masks.

Though we have been trained by reviewers, teachers, and cultural commentators to dislike Collins as much as we are supposed to adore Austen, the stylistics are much the same. Isn't

Collins making the same basic point in a different culture? And doesn't her style help her achieve it? Her deliberate use of excessiveness—the nude in the mirror, the $30k an hour, the Arabian oil tycoon, the not quite legal son. All of these elements show a narratorial smirk, just as Austen does with her "universal truths." If we are looking at two cultures in which women need money from men and their sexuality is their power, then doesn't Collins smilingly imply—given two centuries of increased sexual leniency—a new solution to the situation Austen so delicately paints? And doesn't her particular painting of that sentence work to convey, perhaps in a more historically appropriate way, a similar sentiment?

Of course, there are many who will object to Collins because they object to prostitution, and because of the sex with such young men. Virginia Woolf's opening—"Mrs. Dalloway said she would buy the flowers herself"—is likely appreciated by some of the same people who object to Collins. The role of women appears to be different. Notice how Mrs. Dalloway is *active* in the sentence—in charge of her fate—but notice too that she is still described as a *Mrs.* rather than as "Clarissa Dalloway." This choice shows an awareness of traditional gender roles. The algorithm, by the way, is aware of every time an author uses the word "Mrs." or the word "wife." Out of context all that micro-data might feel like random, superficial information, but in context we can start to see that these small authorial choices can be very important in giving the reader subtle directions on how to read their story. Woolf's use of the title *Mrs.* shows that this author, like the others, is engaged with the question of the cultural relationships between women and men. And Dalloway chooses to buy the flowers *herself* (that old chestnut of a gesture that typically belongs to the stereotypical romantic hero). What defiance of the male patriarchy! Regardless of your personal opinions about prostitution, something similar might be said of Belle Svetlana, née Anabelle Maestro, who is fully in charge and running the most exclusive escort business in New York.

People will debate the role of women in all these books, just as they have in the reception of *Fifty Shades of Grey*—and of course few of us who read will fail to see that as a healthy, sometimes fun and sometimes painful debate. Such conversation is why so many of us read! But the point, whether we like what Belle Svetlana is up to or not, and whether we champion Mrs. Dalloway's buying the flowers herself or not, is that *style* is not to blame here for whether we like the depiction of women or not. The style in all three of these sentences perfectly does the job of an opening sentence that is going to *work*.

Tolstoy's sentence is brilliant in its parallel structure. "Happy families are all alike; every unhappy family is unhappy in its own way." The simplicity on the ear complements the insight brilliantly. And he does what the other writers do in his own unique way: he acknowledges that all novels are about human interactions, that they involve relations filial and familial, and that there must be some sort of unhappiness, or conflict, because otherwise we would have no plot. His opening is not a truth statement, just as the other novelists did not open with truth statements. It is a *fictional* statement, meant to set up the potential of a fictional world. And it signals to any reader, as the other sentences do: here comes a plot!

The best opening sentences—whether reviewers consider

them "highbrow" or "lowbrow," "literary" or "trash," or any other polarizing pair of adjectives—contain all the conflict of a three-hundred-page story in maybe twenty words or less. They achieve this with grammar and with particular usage of the common words that we may hardly notice. Woolf, of course, saw the implied conflict between the title *Mrs.* and the act of buying the flowers herself. If not, she would have used her character's first name, Clarissa. Uh-oh, we may think, if we are new to this novel. Is there a *Mr.*? Is he still present? Is there a conflict? This is nothing more or less smart than understanding structural conventions—from the social to the grammatical—and working them into a potential conflict. This approach works.

Let's look again at Stephen King's line. "Jack Torrance thought: *Officious little prick.*" People who don't like the vulgarity of the word "prick" might object, just as people object to Belle Svetlana's impending sex act. But that doesn't mean the sentence doesn't work. Jack Torrance does like the word, and that tells us something about his world. Again, a novelist's art is to create the illusion of selfhood through style and narration: word choice is part of that, and it should complement grammar, scene, and character. Look how much setup is achieved in six words, three words on either side of the pivotal colon. There is a pleasing rhythm to this structure. The sentence sounds good aloud. It is somehow satisfying. Consider the contrast between the sophistication (or register) of the word "officious" compared to "prick." There is one compelling micro-conflict in the sentence: How are we to take this guy? His language, even in his mind, lends him some kind of presence and authority, which has been the case with every narratorial voice we have met so far. There is another nice conflict between the word "thought" and the hard energy of the word "prick." Why hasn't Jack said it aloud? What has just happened? Why can't he voice his aggravation? Of course King, knowing how to write a winning novel, is throwing us straight into human conflict—two implied characters whose wills are pitted against one another from the first six words. This is the stuff a good stylist needs to recognize: that the first sentence is the hook and the hook is a mixture of voice and conflict achieved through the mechanics of diction and syntax. The job of the text miner with stylometrics is to find the simplest and most reliable way for the computer model to "read" all that complexity and signal when it is being done well.

In the early 1990s, British novelist Martin Amis famously came under fire when he received a reported £500,000 advance in the UK (roughly $850,000) for his next manuscript. At various points in his career, Amis has been considered one of the leading literary writers in England, and he has been praised regularly for his wonderful ability with style. The novel that followed the controversial advance was called *The Information* (1995), a tongue-in-cheek title that nodded to John Grisham's style with *The Firm, The Chamber, The Rainmaker,* and so on, each of which were dominating the charts at the time. The novel received mass media attention and marketing. But it didn't sell, and his publisher later claimed it did not even hit 40,000 in paperback sales. Why? Well, perhaps the first line says it all.

The similarities to Grisham's style stopped with the title. Grisham's novel *The Rainmaker* opens with the sentence: "My decision to become a lawyer was irrevocably sealed when I realized my father hated the legal profession." It has the ingredients (a Grisham opening typically does): an active decision, two characters implied, a reference to the familial bonds of fiction, and conflict at the heart. Simple language, easy to read, no excessive use of clauses. And no unneeded words. We have a believable, authoritative voice. Done.

Amis's novel opens: "Cities at night, I feel, contain men who cry in their sleep and then say nothing." How could we have predicted, just from the first sentence, that this was not a million-copy novel? We will give you one perspective. There is no action here, no interaction, no suggestion of the propulsions of bestselling opening sentences. The line is full of words of emptiness: "night," "sleep," "nothing," with men not able even to witness their own tears. Who is this "I" who is speaking to us? Does his presence command us? Do we feel his authority and authenticity?

It's likely that we don't, and that is because of the style of the sentence. The narrator doesn't "know" (or "realize" as Grisham's narrator does). Instead, he "feels," and he feels parenthetically, inside those two commas—never the strongest way to grab attention with an unusual assertion. He is subordinated grammatically too. His voice, the "I," does not lead the sentence in the active position but comes after the massive facelessness of "cities at night." Where are the human hearts, the multiple characters, the suggested conflict? Where is the power of the sentence? Do we want to chase this "I" through three hundred fifty pages?

Amis's sentence is fine. It is not grammatically unacceptable. It has a certain philosophical quality. Some critics would find literary merit in it. But it doesn't *work* in the same way that the first lines in blockbusters do.

Here are a few more examples of opening lines that do work. All the novels they begin have been bestsellers, and they include both traditionally and self-published authors, so-called lowbrow or mass-market writers, literary writers, and a Pulitzer winner. Would you know which fell into which category?

"Most days I wish I was a British pound coin instead of an African girl."

"The secret is how to die."

"Who wouldn't be skeptical when a man claimed to have spent an entire weekend with God, no less?"

"I was born twice: first, as a baby girl, on a remarkably smog-less Detroit day in January of 1960; and then again, as a teenage boy, in an emergency room near Petoskey, Michigan, in August of 1974."

"They shoot the white girl first."

"She lay on her back fastened by leather straps to a narrow bed with a steel frame."

"Schwarz didn't notice the kid during the game."

"I loved New York with the kind of mad passion I reserved for only one other thing in my life."*

Aren't they all rich and yet simple? Don't they all scream the impression "plot coming!"? Of course style is much more rich and complex than just the first sentence, but that first sentence will often give you a strong sense of how much an author is in control of what is to come, and whether or not he or she has captured the style that will appeal to millions of people.

Christmas Trees

When it comes to computing and measuring style across several thousand novels, things are a lot more complicated than just studying the words in first sentences. As a matter of fact, our analysis of style begins with a collection of several thousand features. These features are mostly common words such as "of," "the," "a," "and," "but," and so on. But we also collect information about syntax, sentence length, punctuation, and parts of speech, along with the information about the most

---

* These opening lines are from Chris Cleave, *Little Bee;* Dan Brown, *The Lost Symbol;* William Young, *The Shack;* Jeffrey Eugenides, *Middlesex;* Toni Morrison, *Paradise;* Stieg Larsson, *The Girl Who Played with Fire;* Chad Harbach, *The Art of Fielding;* and Sylvia Day, *Reflected in You.*

common verbs, nouns, adjectives, and adverbs. We know, for example, how often John Grisham uses an adjective, and whether Danielle Steel or Donna Tartt favors the comma. For each of these features we calculate a measure of the relative frequency within each book. In *The Da Vinci Code*, for example, Dan Brown averages seven instances of the word "the" for every hundred words. John Grisham averages just under six instances per hundred in *The Firm*. If we were given an anonymous book written by either one of these two authors, we would be able to make a pretty good guess at who wrote it based on how often the anonymous book uses the word "the." In Cormac McCarthy's *The Road*, "and" is the second-most frequently occurring word (after "the"), and "he" is the third-most frequent, appearing just under four times per hundred words. The pronoun "she" hardly appears in *The Road*, just one instance for every two thousand words, whereas the pronoun "she" is the seventh-most-frequent word in *The Cuckoo's Calling*, appearing about 1.5 times per hundred. Anthony Doerr's World War II novel, which features both a male and a female protagonist, uses the male and female pronouns "his" and "her" at exactly the same rate (about one occurrence of each for every one hundred words) but in *The Last Boyfriend* by Nora Roberts, "her" is twice as frequent as "his." And while Roberts does not have much use for the second-person pronoun "you," both Nicholas Sparks in *The Notebook* and Adam Johnson in *The Orphan Master's Son* show a fairly strong preference for "you" (1.3 instances per hundred words in Sparks and 1.4 in Johnson). These might seem like tiny details, but the details of fingerprints are as tiny as they are significant.

Our model takes these very basic building blocks of style—not just the foundation stones but the mortar that holds them together—and shows us how every one of them shows up, or not, in all novels. Taken as individual elements, this raw data tells us all sorts of granular things about an author's style—how many commas, how many colons, how many apostrophes and other marks of punctuation, as well as usage of the common words, be they nouns, prepositions, pronouns, or conjunctions. Our data reveals the frequency of the most common and basic verbs such as "did" and "want," the most common of the common nouns such as "woman" and "man," as well as common adjectives and adverbs. At this level, we are not dealing with whether an author is the type to choose a sentence such as "Peter designated the common garden tool that digs, an instrument of weeding the unwanted," or "Peter called a spade a damn useful shovel." But our stylometric analysis can tell us quickly that the first sentence has two instances of "the," a single instance of "that," a single instance of "of," and a single instance of "an" compared to the second sentence that has two "a"s but no "the," no "that," no "an," and no "of." All those articles along with the pronoun and the preposition in the first sentence are dead giveaways about style. The longer-winded expression demands a lot more in terms of foundational apparatus or scaffolding. An author's stylistic signature is calculated from an analysis of these and other similar features in a certain frequency. The frequencies taken as a whole form an author's individual stylistic signal, so they are in J. K. Rowling's pen whether she is writing as Rowling or as Galbraith.

When we fed thousands of books to the bestseller-ometer

and programmed it to focus on these fundamental elements of style, the machine discovered that there are certain habits of style, certain repeated patterns, that are typical to books that make the list. In fact, using only the 491 most frequently occurring words and marks of punctuation, the machine was able to differentiate between bestselling books and non-bestselling books 70 percent of the time. Using only 148 features, the machine guessed correctly 68 percent of the time, and this was just using the most common filler words and punctuation: no nouns, no adjectives, no verbs, no syntax, no sentence data.*

When we studied the results from the model and looked specifically at the features the model had identified as most indicative of bestselling, a number of fascinating things about winning style began to emerge, not the least of which was that women appeared to be doing a much better job when it came to mastering the right words in the right order. Before we come to that, though, first a few observations of a more general nature: The word "do" is twice as likely to appear in a bestseller than in a book that never hit the list. The word "very"—a qualifying word that Strunk and White describe in their classic primer *The Elements of Style* as a "leech" that "infests the pond of prose"—is

---

* By winnowing the data in this manner we avoided the possibility of having an odd feature that totally biased the classifier. Imagine, for example, if every bestselling book used the word "banjaxed" one time and that this word never appeared in any non-bestseller. Our model would quickly learn that this word is a spot-on marker of success. Any author using this word would be predicted to be a bestseller and none of the other features would matter. We avoid this situation by only looking at features that are very common across both the bestselling books and the non-bestselling ones. We force our machine to study the rate at which features appear in both classes of book, and we intentionally omit features that are not present in both classes.

only about half as common in bestselling style as it is in books that don't make it. Strunk and White would approve. The contraction "n't" appears four times more often in books that master the sweet spot of bestselling style than those that don't.

Like the more informal contracted form of "not" as "n't," contractions in general repeatedly show up more in bestsellers. Dropping letters, while it might have been frowned upon in high school, is a good idea in writing popular prose because it helps create that believable, authentic, modern voice that is essential to winning over readers. The narrator's voice, be it third or first person, has to strike readers as real and appropriate if they are going to stay with it. The contraction "-'d" is twelve times more common in bestsellers, while "-'re" is five times more common, along with "'m." We can almost hear Wordsworth calling "yes" from his grave: "yes, the everyday language of the common man." Contemporary bestsellers certainly seem to be nodding in Wordsworth's direction.

Other less formal expressions are popular too. Consider the word "okay." "Okay" appears three times more often in bestsellers. The expression "ugh," a word unlikely to be found in the classics, is also more common. Characters in the bestseller like to ask more questions—we find more question marks in books that hit the list. We do not, however, find more exclamation points; exclamation marks are a negative indicator for bestselling. Top-selling authors know that there is nothing more annoying than something like "It was getting dark! The stairs creaked! Maybe there was a ghost!" The intention behind a doubly expressive "I love you!!" can be much better achieved with "I love you." Plus, no one will want to shoot you.

The ellipsis, used in formal prose to mark an omission, is more common in top novels where it is used not to mark omissions, but as a way to indicate unfinished thought. Readers will typically fill the thought in. "He was wearing that tuxedo again and a six o'clock shadow. Holy crap . . ." Most readers know without further punctuation or words that the "holy crap" here is not a complaint. One of the enjoyments of reading is the feeling a reader has of being very close to the narrator at this moment of ellipsis. In bestselling fiction, the ellipsis is common because it is one way of creating an unspoken understanding between character and reader. Readers like it.

We'll admit that there is a certain fascination to word people like us, with all this data for data's sake. To imagine us staring at a huge spreadsheet together, coffee in hand, mind blown that the word "thing" occurs six times more often in bestsellers than in non-bestsellers, would not be too far off. There are other word lovers who will sit and ponder that fact too. They will wonder, as we did, how this totally nonspecific word, "thing," could be a signal of bestselling fiction. But this study of words is about more than sheer nerdery. It really is. The data can actually tell us something about how the most successful fiction works.

Imagine a scene in which a man is in a bar. He has been unlucky with women. He tells his friend beside him that as a new tactic, he is going to try dating five women at once. The friend chokes on his beer, then responds. Here are two potential comments:

"I would be very surprised if you are still alive after that!"

—or:

"Oh, I'd be really surprised if you're still alive after that."

Which is more natural to the ear, and more effective? Exactly. The latter. Note the big shift in voice and register that comes with those tiny alterations. The period point and the "Oh" replace the exclamation point of the first response—and the deadpan tone of the response comes across easily. Exclamation points, as we noted, are less common in bestsellers, and as this example shows, the tone can be far more nuanced without the loud punctuation at the end. Period points are also more common in winning prose, and both semicolons and colons are significantly less so.

These micro-features of an individual author's style might not be all that revelatory to study as one-off examples, but taken together they show a significant pattern about voice and register in bestselling fiction. The choice to write "I'd" rather than "I would" or "you're" rather than "you are" turns out to be more important than you might think. In bestsellers, adjectives and adverbs are less common, particularly adjectives. What this means is that bestsellers are about shorter, cleaner sentences, without unneeded words. Sentences do not need decorating with additional clauses. Their nouns don't need modifying three times. Verbs, which are a little more common in bestsellers, prefer not to be followed with a string of really very pretty lovely little words ending in -ly. The sentences of the bestseller are not gaudy Christmas trees, carrying the different clashing colors and the weight of lights *and* baubles *and* tinsel *and* angels *and* stars. Better the plain fir tree brought into simple relief.

Men & Women

Using these features, which are so often overlooked, the bestseller-ometer gave us a blueprint for bestselling style. When we took our entire corpus of bestsellers and ranked the books based solely on the criterion of style, we found, quite to our surprise, that the overwhelming majority of the books at the top of the list were by women. This was not the case when we looked at the use of theme or plot. Even though our collection of bestsellers has one hundred more novels by men than women, when it came to mastering the style that is most typical to the bestseller list, women were the clear leaders. Even more arresting, these books that the model ranked best for style were not just by established writers. Many of these women were hitting the list with their first novel. Ten debut books at the top of our ranked style list became instant bestsellers, and nine of them were written by women. We were shocked by the lack of gender diversity at the top of our rankings. Could it be easier to best-sell if you are a woman? Do women have some intrinsic feel for the foundational DNA of bestselling style?

These questions led us down an entirely different path from the one we had started on. The computational study of books throws up many surprises—that's part of the fun of it— and this was a surprise we had to investigate. We wanted to find out just how strong this gender signal was. Prior studies in computational author-gender attribution had achieved accuracies of up to 83 percent, and we wondered if our data would show a similar result.* Could the model really know the difference, just from seeing patterns in things like usage of the word "of" and in the frequency of everyday words like "remember," "myself," and "just," which manuscript was written by a woman and which by a man? Stylometrics has already shown that Robert Galbraith was J. K. Rowling. Could it also tell us that *The Road, The Orphan Master's Son,* and *Hannibal* were all written by men? Would it know that *The Paris Wife, Room,* and *Dead and Gone* all had a female author? When we trained the model to look for a gender signal, we found that the answer in all these cases, and many more, was yes.

Before we discuss what we think this means, we need to point out that our model was not right about every novelist on the list. It correctly guessed author gender 71 percent of the time, and some of the mistakes the machine made are fascinating. One of the most striking errors was that when we asked the model to gender classify all those books it had given high predictions for bestselling, it thought many of the mega-bestsellers written by men were in fact written by women. Three books by James Patterson were near the top of the list of likely bestsellers according to style. All three were incorrectly predicted to be authored by women. *Suzanne's Diary for Nicholas* was one, *Sundays at Tiffany's* was another, and *Four Blind Mice* the last. *Sundays at Tiffany's* may be the easiest to

---

* Matt's work on this was noted in chapter 1, but the key study in the field was completed in 2002 by Sholmo Argamon, Moshe Koppel, and Anat Rachel Shimoni. Their results are reported in a paper titled "Automatically Categorizing Written Text by Author Gender" that appeared in the journal *Literary and Linguistic Computing.*

explain away; Patterson coauthored the book with Gabrielle Charbonnet. If bestselling style really is gendered then perhaps Ms. Charbonnet was responsible for the feminine inflections that the model detected. *Suzanne's Diary for Nicholas* is another matter. As far as we know, Patterson wrote this one by himself, and yet, the model was 99 percent sure that the book was more like the books in our corpus that were written by women. Were it not for the presence of *Four Blind Mice,* then the smoking gun would seem to be genre. Both *Sundays at Tiffany's* and *Suzanne's Diary for Nicholas* are romance novels, and, with apologies to Nicholas Sparks, that genre is dominated by female authors. Genre, however, does not even begin to explain the prediction for *Four Blind Mice.* This book is most certainly not a romance. It is one of Patterson's hard-boiled Alex Cross crime novels. So, what do we make of this? Do we claim that James Patterson owes some part of his enormous success to the fact that he "writes like a woman"? Well, not so fast. Certainly Patterson has mastered the art of writing *for* men and women, and perhaps that has something to do with his style. Certainly the data was telling us *something* about writing style that seemed to correlate to gender. But what exactly was it?

How one goes about interpreting this data is complicated not just by the overall accuracy of the model (which in the case of guessing author gender based on stylistic markers was 71 percent), but also by the individual probabilities assigned to each book. The temptation to make grand and provocative claims can be there—wouldn't it be quite a story to announce that to succeed in the world, at least in fiction, men must be like women?—but in truth the data tells a less sensational and more complex story. Yes, the model was almost certain that *Dolores Claiborne* was written by a woman, and we could imagine a review. ("Patterson and King *both* write like women!") But then take the case of another Stephen King novel, *Mr. Mercedes*. When it came to predicting the likely gender of the author this time, the model thought it could go either way; it predicted that the book was male authored, but only with 50.2 percent probability. A similar result was observed for Diana Gabaldon's novel *Written in My Own Heart's Blood*, which was correctly classified as being female authored, but only with 53 percent probability. So some books might be considered to have a "neutral" style, and in fact it turns out that 25 percent of the books in our collection did not show a strong gender signal one way or the other. Another 25 percent showed only a moderate signal. Fifty percent of the books, however, came back with "gender probabilities" greater than 90 percent. These were worth a closer look.

Of the fifty authors thought to be men with almost total certainty, the model was only wrong about three. Of the top fifty authors that the model most confidently predicted to be female, however, it was wrong about fourteen. These results give two impressions. First, they suggest that the male authors in our corpus have a more consistent and homogenous literary style. Second, it appears that the female authors in our corpus have greater stylistic range. Interesting, but it gets more so.

The three women that the model misclassified as male were Toni Morrison, Sarah Blake, and Barbara Kingsolver. While this could be totally random, we couldn't help but notice that these three women have a few things in common. Toni

Morrison, as well as being a novelist, is a professor. She has won the Pulitzer Prize, the American Book Award, the Nobel Prize, and the Presidential Medal of Freedom. Sarah Blake has a BA from Yale and a PhD from NYU. She teaches writing in various U.S. universities. Barbara Kingsolver has two degrees, has won the Orange Prize for Fiction, the National Humanities Medal, and a Dayton Literary Peace Prize for Distinguished Achievement. These are some of the most traditionally educated and lettered women represented in our corpus—recognized and celebrated leaders in educational and cultural institutions.

Now consider that the top author in terms of paradigmatic male style was Paul Harding, for *Tinkers,* a book that won the Pulitzer Prize. The second author was Charles Frazier for *Cold Mountain,* which won the National Award for Fiction. The third author was Anthony Doerr for *All the Light We Cannot See,* which won the Pulitzer Prize. The fourth author was Cormac McCarthy for *The Road,* which won the Pulitzer Prize. The fifth author is not a Pulitzer winner, but is instead the writer who wrote the *Publishers Weekly* Book of the Year for many years in a row, and who has received awards like the Library of Congress Creative Achievement Award. The author is John Grisham and his book *The Appeal* was next on the list. Were we looking at evidence that seemed to support a claim that the major institutions of literature and letters are coded male, even down to sentence structure?

We looked some more at the backgrounds of these writers. Like the three women on the list, these five award-winning men had some interesting things in common. Harding has a

BA in English and an MFA in creative writing. Charles Frazier holds a PhD in English. Anthony Doerr has a BA in history and an MFA in creative writing. Grisham holds a BS in accounting and a doctorate in law. Of the five, only McCarthy never finished college. He did, however, receive a rather traditional Catholic education in Knoxville after which he enrolled for several years as a liberal arts major at the University of Tennessee. Unsurprisingly, during his time at the university he twice won the Ingram Merrill Award for creative writing.

The more we studied the biographies, the more we began to see that gendered style might just be a false signal. The style that the model was identifying as the most paradigmatically male also appeared to be the most literary: Salman Rushdie and J. R. R. Tolkien were not far away from Frazier and Doerr. Toni Morrison, who was grouped with them, is often regarded as one of the best female literary writers in the U.S. It seemed more likely that we were looking not so much at a "natural" style difference between men and women, but the effect of "nurture" on latent style. It perhaps isn't such a big surprise that the model grouped the novelists, both men and women, who have been thoroughly trained in the traditional canon of English (which incidentally is still fairly male). It also isn't such a surprise that these writers were more "literary" stylists— there is evidence of the literary tradition, and the influence or shadow of the Establishment, in their works and their reception.

What then could we learn from the other end of the list?

The books and authors that the model identified as most

paradigmatically female also turned out to have something in common, but something very different. If the top three men all won the Pulitzer, what did the top three women share? These three writers were Paula Hawkins, Terry McMillan, and Kathryn Stockett. It turns out that all worked in or received degrees in journalism. This trend went deep into the list. Jane Green was a journalist throughout her twenties. Liane Moriarty has a background as a freelance advertising copywriter. Kate Jacobs has a degree in journalism and planned to break into magazine publishing. Lauren Weisberger wrote for various magazines before her breakout. Jessica Knoll was a senior editor at *Cosmopolitan*. Some of the men who were grouped with these female writers have a similar background. James Patterson quit his PhD for a job in advertising. Glenn Beck's background is in radio and TV. The examples go on. The point here is that these writers received a different training in writing and style from those with the MFAs and PhDs in English, and that difference clearly had enough impact to be readily detected by stylometrics.

Learning to write as a copywriter, as a print or Web journalist, or in the world of advertising necessitates an awareness of accessible, colloquial language and style—not Henry James or Herman Melville so much. Magazine journalists are trained in voice, headlines, snappy prose, and the short sentences that work best in the column format of newspapers. Without suggesting that journalistic training necessarily excludes a deep knowledge of the literary canon, or that a journalist can't go on to write a literary novel, it's also likely fair to say that these people have been trained in a style of writing that will appeal to the mass public rather than the Establishment of letters. It is not much of a surprise, then, that the writers in this second grouping are those who have penned some of the instant block-busters of the list. They may not be the literary prize winners but their understanding of style has propelled them into the stratosphere.

While it was true that there were many women at the top of the list when we ordered our library according to "bestsell-ing style," it wasn't *female* style we were observing so much as an aptitude for "the everyday language of the common man" that Wordsworth had implored us to echo. There is a con-temporary trend to the debutantes—not a rule, but a signifi-cant trend. Those writers who appeared to have come from nowhere and then stormed the charts with their novels *The Girl with the Dragon Tattoo, The Girl on the Train, Luckiest Girl Alive, The Friday Night Knitting Club, The Devil Wears Prada,* and *The Help* share a background in journalism. Their novels have stayed on the lists—and not just in the U.S., but globally—for months.

So do King and Patterson "write like women"? No. They write like writers who can write to millions of people. We are glad to observe so many women go from zero to heroine, if you will, with their very first novel. But it's not about gender, not really. It's about an understanding of audience. And it's about a natural feel for language, nurtured by the discipline of their practice.

The Lists: Style

Ten female authors with style

1. Emma Donoghue, *Room*
2. Gillian Flynn, *Dark Places*
3. Emily Giffin, *Something Borrowed*
4. Kate Jacobs, *The Friday Night Knitting Club*
5. Liane Moriarty, *The Husband's Secret*
6. Danielle Steel, *Heartbeat*
7. J. Courtney Sullivan, *Maine*
8. Jeannette Walls, *Half Broke Horses*
9. Jennifer Weiner, *Fly Away Home*
10. Lauren Weisberger, *The Devil Wears Prada*

Ten male authors with style

1. David Baldacci, *First Family*
2. Glenn Beck, *The Christmas Sweater*
3. Harlan Coben, *Six Years*
4. Wally Lamb, *The Hour I First Believed*
5. Michael Connelly, *The Lincoln Lawyer*
6. Chris Culver, *The Abbey*
7. Jonathan Safran Foer, *Extremely Loud and Incredibly Close*
8. James Patterson, *Suzanne's Diary for Nicholas*
9. Matthew Quick, *The Silver Linings Playbook*
10. Nicholas Sparks, *At First Sight*

5

THE **NOIRS,** OR, **WHAT** THE **GIRL NEEDS**

"What's the deal with these girls?"

It was a warm summer day in New York in 2015, and *The Girl on the Train* was still the novel *everyone* was reading. We were having lunch with one of our editors.

"I mean, I can't even imagine not considering a manuscript right now if it has the word *girl* in the title. Should I be making crazy offers on every book with a girl?"

She was only half-serious. But we played with the idea over lunch.

"*Girl with the Dragon Tattoo*. An international hit."

"*Gone Girl*. That was massive."

"*Luckiest Girl Alive*! Where did *she* come from?"

Since 2008, some of the biggest books have been about "those girls." Stieg Larsson had *The Girl with the Dragon Tattoo* in 2008, then *The Girl Who Played with Fire* in 2009, then *The Girl Who Kicked the Hornets' Nest* in 2010. Gillian Flynn took over the literary world with *Gone Girl* in 2012. Then *The Girl on the Train* and *Luckiest Girl Alive* both appeared in 2015. All of them were not "just" *NYT* bestsellers, they were those sort of instant phenomenon books that broke into every reading demographic and almost single-handedly kept some book retailers going. The only comparably huge and recent breakout book without the word "girl" in the title that we could think of was *Fifty Shades of Grey*. Perhaps Anastasia Steele was one of "those girls" too?

No, we decided. She was not. The book wasn't titled *Fifty Shades of That Girl* or *The Girl with the Fifty Shades*. There were good reasons for that.

"Well," said our editor, about the girl novels, "is this random or is it a thing?"

The problem with finding patterns is that if you want to find them you very often will. And when you find one, you will want it to mean something. Copycat publishing works just that way. After *The Girl with the Dragon Tattoo*, there was a vogue for publishing Swedish crime writers across the world. Was being a Swedish male writer the right new discovery in the hunt for finding the next big thing? Well, not really. Some, like Jo Nesbø, made it. Others didn't. Many, many others didn't. Swedish writers weren't the next big thing; they were a crapshoot. Was it that *girl,* then, Lisbeth Salander, Larsson's character, who was the next big thing? Were *girls* the next big thing?

Given the lists since the Dragon Tattoo series, it would be easy to think so. Certainly, at the time of that lunch, the titular girl seemed to be trending. But was this a trend worth investigating? Was it a sign of something significant or was it just opportunistic publishing? We remembered that Larsson, the apparent originator of this trend, didn't actually put a "girl" in his title. Larsson's original title was *Men Who Hate Women*, a phrase that was so disagreeable to the UK publishers that they changed it. It was likely the right decision. There are few fiction readers who would disagree that *The Girl with the Dragon Tattoo* is more alluring than *Men Who Hate Women*, especially given the fact that the majority of fiction readers are female. So perhaps there are several editors out there who, like Larsson's international publishers, suggested that their authors change their titles to include something about a girl. Observing the trend of the moment, maybe any manuscript, whether a thriller, a romance, or a literary experiment, could, in the hands of a savvy publisher, become *The Girl Who . . .* or *Wow, That Girl,* or even *The Girl on the Train.*

That possibility made us cautious. We might have been more inclined to suggest to our editor that she find a manuscript she really liked and then change the title to *Really, This is the Girl,* rather than find a submission with a girl title and then try to like the book.

What's in a Name?

What's in a name? Well for a start, sometimes, ten million dollars. So it is worth thinking a bit about how to get it right. Some bestselling titles refer to physical settings. *Cold Mountain. A Painted House. Black House. Shutter Island. Maine.* We learn something from each of these titles about the prominence and agency of place. A novel set in a black house sounds different in sensibility from one in a painted house. An imaginary trip to Shutter Island is unlikely to lead to the same events unfolding as one that takes place in Maine. If an author points to a place in his title, we expect that place to be a container for an action that would happen differently, or not at all, had all the characters been moved to a different environment. Otherwise, it's not the right title. The place in these novels provides the impetus for the story, or it will if the novel is well named and well written. By the end of such a novel, we will feel an intimacy with the fictional place as though it's its own voiceless character.

Bestselling titles might also capture an event, and we can presume that if an event makes the title page it is not just a plot point but something that provides the story with a more fundamental structure and meaning. *Accident* is one such title. *Death Comes to Pemberley. Fall of Giants. One Day. The Kiss. A Visit from the Goon Squad.* Nothing will be the same before or after *that* moment, *that* day, *that* kiss, *that* accident. The fate of the characters is to respond, to react, to reacclimatize. But the characters are not the primary agent: the event is bigger than they are.

More common to the lists than either of these kinds of titles are ones that point to *things,* to objects, typically common nouns. Sometimes these things are qualified by a specifying word. Not just *Tears* but *Dragon Tears.* Not *The Inheritance* but *The Boleyn Inheritance.* Not any old *Code,* but *The Da Vinci Code.* Other times two common nouns are put into a relationship that brings questions to the reader's mind. *Water for Elephants. Dragonfly in Amber. Memories of Midnight.* Why don't the elephants have water? What's special about the preserved dragonfly? Who is reminiscing about midnight? Most effectively, perhaps, is the noun that stands alone, enticing: *The Goldfinch; The Firm; The Circle.* Titles with "The" are much more common on the lists than titles with "A." Does *A Goldfinch* sound right? No. *A Hit?* No. *A Lost Symbol?* No.

The specificity of the word "The" asks us to trust that *this* goldfinch has more relevance—enough to hold an entire story symbolically, emotionally, or structurally—for more than three hundred pages. So, *The Gift, The Christmas Sweater, The Notebook.* The only time "A" works better than "The" is when the noun is so unusual and specific that the generality of the word "A" lends it some grander, more universal, or metaphorical sense. The use of "A" widens the potential: *A Spool of Blue Thread; A Thousand Splendid Suns; A Dog's Purpose; A Game of Thrones.*

Sometimes an author will choose to have neither a definite nor an indefinite article. These titles, with their lack of specificity to an individualized thing, use nouns in a more thematic, metaphorical sense: *Beautiful Ruins; Bag of Bones; Beach Music; Freedom; Disclosure; Heart of the Matter.* Effective? Yes, perhaps. But "The" remains the most successful way to begin a title because it is a word that implies agency focused somewhere, be that focus on a place, on an event, on an object, or somewhere else. The title gives us a clue about how to relate to the story that follows.

When it comes to titles like *Gone Girl,* though, we are being directed to character as focus and agent. One-fifth of all the bestsellers in our collection have titles that point to a character. Rarely, however, does the title give us an eponymous hero or heroine. There are a few. *Dolores Claiborne. Olive Kitteridge. Hannibal. Cross. Scarpetta. Zoya.* These titles suggest a character study, the journey of, or fascination with, a character who is compelling enough to carry the whole novel. They suggest we will learn about this particular individual in some psychological fullness and that that fullness will carry the plot. Titles of this sort, with specific given names, were far more common during the rise of the novel in the eighteenth and nineteenth centuries. *Pamela. Moll Flanders. Emma. Madame Bovary. Tom Jones.* If we find a first name today, it is more often than not qualified: *Defending Jacob; Loving Frank; Gerald's Game; Kill Alex Cross; Still Alice; The Key to Rebecca.* In all these cases, the titles imply more than a character study. The character name is being associated with some fundamental element of the plot: the two together create the story.

Character titles, however, are much more commonly concerned with a protagonist's role or status rather than their given first name. Of our hundred bestselling titles that point to character, the majority introduce someone's role, be that professional or sociocultural. Sometimes these roles carry so much import that they need no qualifying adjective. What would it mean to be that individual who finds himself in the role of *The Alchemist, The Ghost,* or *The Martian*? Not just *an* alchemist, which is intriguing enough, but *the* alchemist. Clearly there's a story here because these are such unusual roles.

In other cases, the role itself seems less remarkable: *The Historian; The Piano Teacher; The Postmistress; The Client.* Here the

"The" makes it *this* piano teacher among many, or *that* client. The use of the definite article empowers that specific person, even in an everyday role. It loads the character with potential. We know we are to read about the relationship between a full, rounded character like Iris and the role of the postmistress that she finds herself in. Therein will lie the conflict, or the irony. In this instance, Iris is *the* postmistress because she violates her role: she steals a letter and does not deliver it. She is therefore singled out. Not *a* postmistress, but *the* postmistress. The one who did it, who acted, who became the agent of plot. The title, then, when well chosen, should foreground the agency and, therefore, the action and drama of the entire upcoming narrative—its structure, its focus, its drive, its magnetism. If we recognize this, we can see that the vogue for girl titles is likely about more than just titles that sound good to the ear. They are part of a trend of recent headline-grabbing novels that put women and their traditional roles front and center.

When it comes to sociocultural roles, the word "wife" is popular in bestselling titles, but it is always qualified. The title is not just *The Wife*. She has more to contend with than this. Titles about a woman in marriage that hit the lists are titles such as *The Silent Wife, The Paris Wife, A Reliable Wife*. The names of these novels are meant to make us wonder what happens to this woman when put in relationship to Paris, to silence, to reliability as well as, given what "wife" implies, to her husband. How do her options and her likely conflicts change? Who is the contemporary woman in this role? The same question is latent in all the "girl" bestsellers. Notably, "husband" only appears in one title in our collection, and rather than being qualified by an adjective (to make her *be* something), this husband *has* something, and it's not necessarily a good thing to have. *The Husband's Secret.* Uh-oh. A secret in marriage? There's the hook, and any quick look at the bestseller list will tell you that troubled marriage appears to be a big hook for the reading market at the moment. The books making the lists are evidence of our contemporary fascination with the roles of women in their place in the family, in marriage, and in the public sphere. Hence, wives more than husbands and girls more than boys.

In our collection of bestsellers, there are ten books with the word "girl" in their title. But before we can recommend that our editor start buying up girl books, we have to understand who is the right kind of girl. And the right kind of girl, ironically, is the wrong kind of girl. *A Girl to Come Home To* is different, isn't it, from *The Girl Who Played with Fire*? The first title did not best-sell even after rerelease, which at the time of this writing had sold 117 copies according to Nielsen's BookScan. The second title, of course, is one of Larsson's mega-hits. *A Girl to Come Home To* is different from a *Gone Girl*. Why? Well, why be the static girl sitting at home, when you can be playing, and playing with fire of all things? Which is more intriguing? Why be the girl *to come home to* when you can be the girl who is already *gone*? Why be *The Girl on a Swing*, frankly—and she was another non-bestselling girl—when you can be *The Girl on the Train*? One goes nowhere; the other has possibilities. The difference between all of these pairs is the difference for readers between a two-star and a five-star review. The girl who makes it to the list is a funny kind of girl, a new heroine in mass culture. She is not the sweet child. She is displaced. A misfit. She's angry. This girl is the feminine noir.

Of course there is a powerful irony here. Readers tend to think of the blockbuster hero or heroine as someone full of agency, full of drive—someone compelling and special enough to hold our attention. We expect that this character can and will have the capacity to see the light and dark in the world and survive. But doesn't the word "girl" carry a very different implication? Doesn't "girl" suggest someone young, innocent, and dependent on adults? Someone not yet in control of her own destiny. Someone who needs nurturing and protection. But the girls who are all over the lists right now—and they are not in fact girls at all—are not like this sort of girl, and they stay there week after week. The question of their agency is central—central to their stories, to the way we interpret them, and to the global reviews that feature them.

Character Is Destiny

Several times in this book we have asked what readers want. Many claim they read for theme, or for genre. And it is likely true that many keep reading because certain plotlines are strangely addictive. But when they are reviewing or attending book clubs, thousands of readers claim that actually character is likely the most important aspect of the difference between a good novel and a can't-put-down novel. It is through characters that we can observe vicariously or judge quietly, or fantasize unnoticed. So many of us buy novels for the promise of these experiences. Characters take us to new places—geographic, emotional, mental, moral, sexual. We can have, for the duration of the novel, a wicked mother, when perhaps in reality we have a caring one. We can have or be an adulterous lover when we may in fact have or be a faithful one. We can, while we escape into reading, fly to the moon, murder people, and marry Heathcliff. Part of the joy of reading is how we position ourselves alongside or in opposition to characters—or sometimes both—as they show us potential results of crime or lust or commitment or faith or daring. Characters make us think and rethink. They bring us something new. Some characters even have their own fan clubs, and inspire fan fiction, and T-shirts and even, in the case of Harry Potter, an entire theme park in Florida. But many fiction writers, when asked to teach or write about how to "do" character, admit that character is the most difficult aspect of fiction both to master and to teach.

The whole concept of literary character has been surrounded with theoretical controversy, most of which would strike the average sensible reader as a load of nonsense. It is basically a fight between a few different positions. The first and most simple is that characters, to be thought of as successful, must be so unique, so complex, and so well rendered inside and out that the reader can know them in a way they will never know their real friends or even themselves. In other words, a character in a novel should be psychologically deep and real.

Other understandings of character argue that a character is something that stands in one particular gender, social, or cultural role in relation to other possible roles. Therefore a character takes its meaning from the fact, perhaps, that she is the little orphan "girl" and not the old rich baron. Both are defined by the other and by the roles the other is forced into. So we get *Beauty and the Beast* or *Lady and the Tramp*. In this understanding of character, the psychology of one is less important than the structural positions the different characters occupy and what we learn, through them, about agency in the whole system. The protagonists of the recent girl novels, because they are not typical girls, disrupt the tired and typical positions in the system. This disruption of our expectations results in characters who are both internally complex and outwardly challenged. They are different and, accordingly, must act differently. The key to understanding what makes these characters work, or not work, is found in their agency.

Strong characters always have agency. They have some version of power, motivation, drive. What they do with it and what stands in their way is what character-driven novels are all about. But character is hard to get at, and the point of raising any of the theoretical controversy about character is simply to show that literary critics and writers alike disagree about how character is and should be made. We have to be aware of this when we start thinking about creating a computer model that can understand character.

There are certain tools and tricks good novelists can play with when they create their characters. Some authors rely heavily on description. Say we want to turn our editor into a character, and we will since she was the one who started this conversation. We might begin our novel, titled *The Girl on Floor Sixteen,* like this:

> Daniela sat behind her desk in the Flatiron Building sur-
> rounded by hardcover books and manuscripts. The light
> from the window behind her reflected in the shine of her
> chin-length chestnut hair. She wore a white shirt, smartly
> buttoned.

And so on.

So far, we can know Daniela only from the objects around her. The shirt tells us something. So does the building she is sitting in. Some authors do a lot of this descriptive work to create character. Others, however, may rely heavily on dialogue. Thus, it would matter at this point if Daniela's assistant came into her office and said to her: "Madam, would it be at all possible if I took a four- or five-minute break to call my sick mother?" It would equally matter if the assistant said nothing of the sort, but instead said, "Hey Boss, I'm skipping out to go see Mom." They both give us a very different impression of the girl in our story.

Free indirect discourse, which is when a narrator enters a character's mind, is another trick. Some authors use it all the time—Jane Austen was the expert. Others are noisy in their dislike of it. In our evolving story about the girl on floor sixteen, free indirect discourse might look something like this: "Daniela looked up at her assistant. Was she ever going to shut up about her insipid mother and find her a new manuscript about a girl?" At this moment, the narrator has stolen the thoughts of Daniela's inner mind and shared them. We learn a little more about her.

The important thing to notice from the perspective of the literary critic and text miner, is that so far, Daniela herself has done nothing at all. She is static, passive, subject to a gaze. She will only really come alive, and become someone to her readers, when she acts. When she responds, moves, speaks, reads, frowns, or smiles. She needs to *do* something. When Daniela acts she sets the plotline moving, and when she acts again and again she starts manipulating its trajectory and its curves. Her actions will be a key component in creating an attractively shaped plotline like some of the ones in chapter 3. Therefore our notion of character, among the many to choose from, is that a character must do things, and that doing is their agency. The novelist can really only do this very well with verbs. "Daniela was happy" is different from "Daniela laughed." Both of those are different from "Daniela beamed." Verbs are key. In *The Da Vinci Code,* Robert Langdon *fears* tight spaces. Jason Bourne *kills* people in *The Bourne Ultimatum.* Amy *plans* a complex revenge against her *cheating* husband, Nick, in *Gone Girl.* The Borg in *Star Trek assimilate.* Obviously there are other things about character that give us clues about who they are: their looks, their gender, their race, and so on, but until we see them act we really don't know them. The question for our research was whether or not certain verbs, certain actions, sell better than others. More specifically we wondered whether there were winning patterns associated with the actions and agency granted to male and female characters. What we found is that there were both.

Do Something!

From a computational perspective, character is a very tough nut to crack. Theme, as we saw in chapter 2, can be reliably mined from a novel because themes are signaled by nouns, and nouns are a relatively easy class of words for a machine to identify. Because of the various ways novelists inscribe character, it is far more difficult for a computer to identify the characters in a novel than the themes, and it is even more difficult for the machine to figure out what those characters are doing. The most obvious complication is that authors don't always refer to their characters by name. *Fifty Shades of Grey* is a first-person narrative, and Anastasia is most frequently identified as "I," not as "Anastasia" or as "Ms. Steele" as Christian likes to call her. Lisbeth Salander in *The Girl with the Dragon Tattoo* is sometimes "Lisbeth," sometimes "Salander," sometimes "she," and occasionally "her." And it is entirely possible that someone called Lisbeth could appear in a novel as "Liz" or "Beth" or even "Betty." So, that creates one big headache.[*] A second complication involves pronouns. Novels have multiple characters—lots of different *he*s and *she*s that create a problem of disambiguation. So, in

---

[*] Teaching a machine to understand all of these possible variations of a name is probably impossible. We say "probably" because there are some very smart people working on exactly these kinds of disambiguation problems. This branch of research is called "Named Entity Recognition" (NER), and like many other methods we have employed in this book, NER is a subspecialty within the field of natural language processing. Interested readers may wish to consult Bamman, Underwood, and Smith's paper titled "A Bayesian Mixed Effects Model of Literary Character," which can be found in the 2014 *Proceedings of the 52nd Annual Meeting of the Association for Computational Linguistics,* pages 370–379.

Gone Girl, for example, we have the problem of how to figure out which instance of *she* refers to the lead female Amy and which *she* is Boney, the detective. Human beings do this sort of disambiguation easily enough by understanding the context in which those *she*s are occurring. For computers, this is a much more difficult task.*

We found that we could understand a great deal about character agency by training our computer to locate instances of character names as well as instances of pronouns and then collect the verbs associated with those characters and pronouns. Using this data about how characters act in a novel—whether Daniela stands, or whether she reads, for instance—we were able to predict whether a novel in our corpus was a bestseller or not with 72 percent accuracy. That was just from the basic verbs, one data point of the bestseller-ometer taken in isolation. From this data, we learned what bestselling characters do that non-bestselling characters don't do. Everyday verbs really make a difference.

---

* Even though we now have algorithms that are very good at identifying character names in a text, figuring out who's who and who is doing what largely remains an unsolved problem. Despite these difficulties, new research under way in Matt's lab at the University of Nebraska is showing that some aspects of character agency can be reliably extracted. Over the past two years, Matt and his student team in the Nebraska Literary Lab have been developing and prototyping a method for detecting and extracting character agency data in order to study the depiction of male and female characters in nineteenth-century fiction. Their paper titled "Understanding Gender and Character Agency in the 19th Century Novel" is currently under review. While the goal of the research in Matt's lab is quite different from ours, we found we could employ the Nebraska method in our examination of bestsellers. Using this approach, we processed our corpus of bestsellers in order to identify every pronoun and character name along with the verbs associated with each. We then ran a series of classification experiments in order to evaluate the strength of the verb-to-pronoun associations but also to explore whether there was a relationship between certain pronoun-verb pairings and bestselling.

Regardless of whether the character is male or female, best-selling protagonists have and express their *needs*. These protagonists *want* things, and we learn about those wants. The verbs *need* and *want* are the two biggest differentiators between selling and not selling—it is remarkable that characters in less successful books are markedly less likely to be described with reference to needs and wants. The bestselling novel is a world in which characters know, control, and display their agency. Their verbs are clean and self-assured. Characters in bestsellers more often *grab* and *do*, *think* and *ask*, *look* and *hold*. They more often *love*. These characters have some self-awareness and self-knowledge. They own themselves, even when they don't necessarily like themselves. They live their lives; they make things happen. The bestselling character, whether male or female, *tells*, *likes*, *sees*, *hears*, *smiles*, and *reaches*. This is someone with energy. This is someone who *pulls* and *pushes*, someone who *starts*, *works*, *knows*, and, ultimately, *arrives*. Those characters who inhabit the *NYT* bestseller list are typically ones with direction, capacity, and surety. None of these verbs feature as frequently in the novels that did not hit the lists.

Compare a character who acts in these self-assured ways to a second kind of character who does very little of the above. Our model would show us that this second character does not engage in very much *needing*, *wanting*, *doing*, *telling*, or *arriving*. Instead, the character that readers find far less attractive, is much more inclined to do things like *halt* and *drop*. Readers appear not to devote their leisure time to that second kind of character in fiction who *demands*, who *seems*, who *waits*, and who *interrupts*. Readers want someone to *be* not to *seem*. They want someone to *do* not to *wait*. They want more confidence and grace than the character who *demands* and *interrupts*. The less successful character, whether male or female, too often *shouts, flings, whirls*, and *thrusts*. Exhausting! These less successful characters tend to *murmur, protest*, and *hesitate*. Readers roll their eyes—these are the verbs of a flailing child not a starring lead. The adage *he who hesitates is lost* applies to fiction too, both to him and her. Hesitation doesn't keep pages turning. If you're in the position of agency, and you too often *halt, drop*, or *hesitate*, you'll create only blank pages.

The data does show some differences between the gender roles of men and women in novels that hit the list. Both characters act, they *do* something. But there are differences in the actions of the male and female characters that tend to appear and reappear on the lists. Both men and women *spend, walk*, and *pray* more than characters who don't sell well. But men do most of the *kissing*, whereas women do more of the *hugging*. Men *fly, drive*, and *kill* more than the women do. Women *talk, read*, and *imagine* more often than the men. He *travels;* she *stays*. He *assumes;* she *decides*. He *promises;* she *believes*. They both *love*—and love is not a feminized action on the lists— but, of the two, she is the more likely to *hate*. Both characters *see*, but he is the one who *stares*. Often at her. She *screams* and *shoves*. He *worries* and *punches*. There is a pattern of traditional gender roles on the bestseller lists, even stereotypical ones, but these men and women have other notable things in common that tell us more about how successful fiction works.

When we looked at all the verbs that have to do with mental and emotional states across our collection, we found that the range of existential experience was much greater in bestsellers. There were twenty-two verbs that appear significantly more often in bestsellers than in other novels, and those other novels had only eight repeated verbs that mark them as a category. Four of the top verbs to describe the mental and emotional expression of bestselling characters are *need, want, miss,* and *love.* The possible journeys between just those four verbs have led to many classic and mega-bestsellers on the lists. On average, bestselling characters "need" and "want" twice as often as non-bestsellers, and bestselling characters "miss" and "love" about 1.5 times more often than non-bestsellers.

The mental and emotional state of the characters in less-selling books is likely best described as passive. These verbs suggest a passive engagement with their circumstances, giving the impression that for these characters it would be truer to say that the world creates them rather than they create their world. These are people who are also less open, and slightly more negative. They *accept, dislike, seem, suppose,* and *recover* themselves. They also *wish,* which is the more passive and re-signed version of the bestselling verbs *need* and *do.* On average, non-bestselling characters "wish" 1.3 times more often than characters in bestsellers. Non-bestselling characters do some sort of "supposing" 1.6 times more often than their winning counterparts, and they "dislike" things almost two times more often than bestselling characters.

When we put them under the microscope, the patterns in verbs that describe physical action are no more complimentary for the lower-selling character. We start to think he may bring his fate on himself, not just in the novel but in the literary marketplace, too. "Character and fate are two words for the same thing," said the German philosopher Novalis. Heraclitus, the Greek philosopher, said: "A man's character is his fate." Consider, then, the likely fate of a character who *grunts, clutches, peers, gulps, flushes, trembles,* and *clings.* This is hardly the archetypal hero, not in any culture. Imagine watching him or her. Has the person been poisoned? Is she having a heart attack, perhaps? How about if he also *jerks, shivers, breaks, fumbles,* and *flings?* This person appears not to know his proverbial (or literal) ass from his elbow. Such a character is not going to best-sell.

There is something altogether more attractive about a character whose body makes more simple and controlled gestures. The bestselling character *eats, nods, opens, closes, says, sleeps, types, watches, turns, runs, shoots, kisses,* and *dies.* Actually, male and female characters *die* and *survive* with equal frequency in the bestseller—though those who are dying and surviving are not necessarily the lead roles. The important thing to note is that in the bestselling novel *someone* is often doing something as dramatic as surviving or dying, and they are not, as their lesser-selling friends prefer, *yawning.*

Most bestselling characters have something magnetic about them that makes them stand out from the crowd. They are gifted in some way, able to achieve what others can't. Mitch McDeere in *The Firm* is handsome, Harvard trained, a relentless thinker and workaholic, and he doesn't need sleep. He can outwit the mob and the FBI, and at the same time. Then there is Susie Salmon in *The Lovely Bones.* She's dead. But also isn't dead. From "her heaven," Susie has omniscience and is able to watch the investigation into her murder from all angles. She can even borrow someone's body to complete her love story. Robert Langdon is no simple scholar in tweed. Deciphering the Da Vinci Code takes more than a few library books and a cup of tea: he is the brilliant, quick-thinking symbologist and the best in the world. Amy Dunne's type A personality in *Gone Girl* may lead her to murder, but we don't miss that she's a master liar with a master plan; she outsmarts everybody in a way that could make a reader's hair curl. Lisbeth is a master hacker. Without her, there is no solution to the mysteries of *The Girl with the Dragon Tattoo*. No one knows code like she does. The same is true of Pulitzer Prize bestsellers. Young Werner in *All the Light We Cannot See,* for example, uses his prowess with electronics to escape the orphanage while Marie-Laure achieves a certain heroism even though she is blind. What do these and so many other bestselling characters have in common? None are wishers, supposers, or yawners. They are special. They are courageous and confident. And readers support them.

Bestselling characters not only do the right things in the right way, they also speak in the right way. The data on dialogue tags tells us that if you are a reader of heroines, for example, you likely won't favor her if she *begins, speaks, accepts, remarks, exclaims, mutters, answers, protests, addresses, shouts,* or *demands*. There might be a few cheap jokes to be made about women there ("Methinks she doth protest too much!" would be a start), but really these verb choices are about effective and ineffective characterization. The fact that not so many novels with women who shout and demand make it onto the lists has nothing to do with any implied portrayal of women in our culture. It just means that any words that a writer may choose to express the sentiment of "she said" that are not simply those very words "she said" are one of the writerly roads into hell. She *asked* is an exception, since it acknowledges a question. Any wannabe bestselling authors who have bothered to pick up a manual on style, who have been to an English class beyond middle school, or who have trained themselves by reading other talented and successful writers, have learned that endless adverbs and strings of adjectives are like sticking fat tires and flashing rims on a vintage Jaguar. Similarly, the way in which a character is speaking should be established through context and not conspicuous, inauthentic, gratuitous verbs that make a character appear to have lost their plot. Consider these two options. First:

> It was 7:30 p.m. and Daniela was still at her desk. On her way out, her assistant told her that she had four calls to return, a cover to approve, and three printed manuscripts waiting for her attention. "I love you too," she said.

Second:

> It was 7:30 p.m.: a long day. Daniela's assistant walked into her office.

> "You have four phone calls to return, a cover to approve, and three printed manuscripts waiting," he decried.

> "I love you too," Daniela announced.

What? It's almost the same message, but the second version makes little sense because the way the speech is rendered knocks all the clues about tone out of whack. The first gives us a wry sarcasm; the second suggests Daniela is delirious. But so many amateur writers are this overexuberant about their speech tags.

The computer model is as clear as most writing professors, and is unanimous in its support of them. When writing direct speech, the dialogue tags should be almost silent to the reader's ear, as unremarkable as the word "said." The contextual setup and the words inside the quotation marks matter to effective characterization, not a distracting verb outside them. This is precisely why *ask* and *say* are bestselling verbs but *demanded* and *exclaimed* are not.

Heroine Noir

Why is *need* the top verb to differentiate bestsellers from non-bestsellers? How come *wish* is *need*'s equivalent in books that don't sell? It's a marked difference in the data. Well, we thought, *I think, therefore, I am. I wish*, therefore, I sit and wait for something to happen. I *need*, therefore, I act. Action drives plot. The character who identifies a need has to move into journey, movement, interaction, and possibly conflict. The kinds of needs they have and how they handle them tell us who they are.

When it comes to "the girls," the bestseller-ometer told us that the new girls on the list are not passive. Not at all. They need. They want. They act on both as far as they are able to. *The Girl with the Dragon Tattoo, Gone Girl*, and *The Girl on the Train* do verbs very well. And the machine scores showed that it is the girls in particular, and not the men in the novels, who drive success. Did Lisbeth sell all those copies of *Dragon Tattoo*? As far as the model is concerned, yes she did. It wasn't the whodunnit plot. It wasn't the Swedish setting. It wasn't the brutal scenes of rape. It wasn't the male detective figure. It was her. And Lisbeth definitely started something. There is definitely something to the current trend for a certain kind of girl, the darker, more shadowed feminine that would never appear in, say, a Debbie Macomber novel.

How can we claim this? Or at least, how can we bring more support to those reviewers in the press who, when pushed to explain the success of Stieg Larsson, wrote that it was likely a character book and not, as other critics argue, a plot or genre book? In each novel, we measured the verbs attached to the first-person pronoun "I," and those attached to male and female pronouns. The likelihood of being based on the work of male characters alone was only 29 percent in *The Girl with the Dragon Tattoo*. So Blomkvist is not the standout character. The model thought he was forgettable, and frankly, having read the book ourselves when it was released, we find that we have mostly forgotten him too. But we have not forgotten Lisbeth. When we looked at the other girl novels, we found the same pattern, but not as pronounced. The men in *Gone Girl* got a 72 percent score for being likely bestsellers, and in *Girl on the Train* it was 97 percent. This high number suggests that Paula Hawkins had her male characters making the right moves, but it's worth recognizing the fact that they have much less presence in this novel than in the other two, and therefore less chance of displaying the wrong kind of agency. However, while the men in *The Girl on the Train* definitely give a strong signal, the female characters outperform them, as they do in all of these girl novels. Female agency in *The Girl with the Dragon Tattoo* scored 93 percent and 99 percent in both *Girl on the Train* and *Gone Girl*. So the model showed yes, clearly there is something to these girls.

The data seem surprising, given the kind of girls these characters are, so apparently different from the traditional idealized feminine. We are a long way from the feminized beauty, grace, and goodness of a Danielle Steel heroine. But given how these shadowy girls have stormed the international bestseller charts in quick succession, they must be showing us a cultural thirst for something—for some kind of adventure, or probing, or escape. Undoubtedly, sociologists would have much more to say along these lines: from our domain in literary criticism we are looking at the mainstream rise of a new subgenre. Dubbed the "domestic noir," this genre is all about a new kind of female heroine, the girl. This girl is significant because she is the vehicle for bringing the traditional elements of the thriller, the whodunnit—even the horror—into the private sphere. Typically these darker plots take place outside of the sanctity of the home. They happen in the public sphere, the place of spies and governments, courtrooms and jails, in schools and offices. In the domestic noir, the girl takes us into the household, into the realms that are traditionally and stereotypically hers. She takes us into a relationship, into marriage and into family, and she turns all the stereotypes on their heads. In all these spaces, this new heroine appears either as avenging angel, angry victim, or violent agent of destruction.

This girl in some sense is about purification. She is there to test, to battle with and displace the constrictions and expectations placed on women. She is one instance of the purification that is part of the work of thousands of bestselling characters in different genres. Many heroes and heroines are those agents who are able to bring, usually with some struggle, purification to their fictional world. Watching them achieve this is likely one of the cathartic pleasures of reading. The cultural anthropologist Mary Douglas gives us an apt metaphor. In her work, she talks about systems and anomalies, and explains a very human desire to name something in a way that enables that person or group of people to respond to it in a certain way. In a system where monogamy is the accepted norm, we can call someone a "swinger" in order not to condemn his choice to sleep with people other than his partner. Governments that perceive a threat to their security might be inclined to label possibly menacing individuals as terrorists in order to sanction a drone attack. Naming is very important to what we allow and will not allow. This is true of everything from the title of novels to personal and political decisions, and it is also central to literary art.

For Mary Douglas, naming is part of the process of expelling a threat, named or unnamed. The perceived "problems" in a healthy system might be literal or metaphorical dirt, pollution, or perhaps a taboo. They might be a controversial new idea, a progressive pattern of behavior, or a murderer on the loose in a small American town. Of course all fictional plots have their perceived "pollutions"—they are as old as the wicked stepmother who stands between the beautiful girl and the prince.

The recent girls on the lists are interesting partly because they challenge this kind of labeling. Douglas makes the point that nothing is *intrinsically* an anomaly or "dirt," but it is treated as such if it does not fit the cultural system in which it is experienced. There is nothing so very different about Lisbeth Salander with her spiked punk hair and tattoos, at least not until she is compared to the norm, both within her fictional Swedish setting and as one female character in a history of female literary heroes. Lisbeth is fascinating because she is both the perceived "problem" and the solution. The same is true of Rachel in *The Girl on the Train* and Amy in *Gone Girl*. All three are part of more complex and gripping narratives than the standard and stereotypical good vs. evil plot. These girls are somehow all of it—the good, the bad, the problem, and the solution. What do we do with the dark feminine, the troubled girl?

Think for a minute about the bestselling hero of this generation. No book about bestsellers can likely feel complete without him. Harry Potter. In the Harry Potter series, the dirt in the system—the evil—is even referred to as "He-Who-Must-Not-Be-Named." So, unnamed, he lives on. This is the most literal example in recent bestselling fiction of what Douglas describes. It is only Harry himself who dare name the "dirt." He repeatedly and brazenly uses the moniker of his arch-nemesis, Lord Voldemort, to the trembles and shushing of the rest of the characters. And it is of course Harry and Harry alone who has the power to fight him and ultimately, after seven books with seven battles, expel him from the system not just at Hogwarts but in the whole Muggle (non-wizard) world, too. Thus returns order, safety, and, of course, *marriage*. The final epilogue brings marriage to all good wizards involved in the series, and thus the history-making, record-breaking literary franchise ends with the phrase "All was well." This sentiment is so common in best-selling narratives that it reflects a cultural if not a global psychological need.

The "All was well" resolution seems like a requirement of narrative—an essential part of the three-act structure. It is not always achieved, of course, but stories do seem to be propelled forward until they find a sense of closure and stillness. Character is absolutely embroiled in that propulsion. Harry starts out a loner or a misfit, a boy with a zigzag scar on his head who lives under a flight of stairs. In his teenage years he finds himself suddenly the chosen one. As the most gifted wizard, his days are then spent making things disappear and reappear, overcoming talking shape-shifting dogs, flesh-eating plants, hexes, and soul-sucking death eaters, beating all others at Hogwarts' sport of lacrosse on a broomstick, and even returning from death. After all this drama, all the specialness, Harry's story ends in a fairly conventional middle-class arrangement by any of our standards. The perfect last act for the hero of a decade was, we find out, to propose to a nice, pretty family girl, the sister of his best friend. When we get to Rowling's final pages, the most powerful and adventurous good wizard of modern-day literature appears to have done something like move to suburbia to raise an SUV full of children, eat home cooking, and read the newspaper. The dirt in the system at Hogwarts has been cleansed: without his nemesis in opposition to him Harry appears no longer to be provoked into heroism. In averageness the story cannot go on: there is no further narrative compulsion. The story finds its stillness. All is well.

So many bestsellers can be understood in the same way. By the end of the Fifty Shades series, the master of kinky fuckery with commitment issues is in a meadow under the sun with his wife and children. At the end of *The Da Vinci Code,* the threat of Opus Dei is overcome, and after the high drama of the plot-line, the final scenes have Robert and Sophie unexpectedly meet part of her family, who carry the sacred Christian bloodline. The book ends with a return to family, and a suggestion of future romance between Robert and Sophie. All is well. There are examples of this kind of closure all over the list—it may not always be happy, but a sense of resolution and stillness is typically part of the narrative contract that works.

Some characters, however, are just never going to get there. The girls don't make it because they are the dirt and the solution in one. They threaten the traditional mores of the system, but they are also the figures who will expose the guilt of others in an attempt to purify the world they see around them. As agents of change they are at once powerful and limited. This is why they are called "girls"—it is important that the author points to the problem of their limited agency. Until authors find the right solution and place for this dark girl figure, we predict she will keep turning up on the bestseller lists.

Bestselling Hat Trick

We have said that *need* is the most influential verb for our model in finding a bestseller, and that needs show character. Let's take

Gone Girl as the example. When we pull out all the sentences of the novel in which the characters express need, we get a snapshot of the plot and tone of the book in 163 sentences. Amy and Nick's use of the word *need* captures their marriage perfectly, and to read a spreadsheet of these extracted sentences is to quickly experience the mounting tension between them. Nick says, "I need a drink." Amy says, "I needed to be ambushed, caught unawares, like some feral love-jackal." Nick says, "I don't feel the need to explain my actions to her." Amy says, "I am a girl who is very bad, and I need to be punished." Nick says of his wife: "She needed to dazzle men and jealous-ify women." It goes on. Their contempt for each other creates the emotional tension of the story, and shows us the dark side of their marriage. All the needs in the novel, in fact, point to the dark side, to the emotional and psychic underbelly of a marriage gone sour. It culminates, when Nick realizes she is a serious threat, and says, "I needed other people to back me up—that my wife wasn't amazing Amy but avenging Amy."

There is so much that could be said about these three "girl" novels—they warrant a book of criticism of their own. The figure of this dark feminine in mass culture could become a whole PhD research topic. For our purposes here, we will just say that the computer model shows us three aspects of these novels that can help explain their success. The agency of the characters, especially the female characters, is the first of these three things. The second is about plot, or what we have called the curves of strong sales. The third is about theme, and specifically that central theme of human closeness that we discuss in chapter 2. These three novels weave these elements of fiction together in such a way as to hit a sweet spot, and we know from the sales figures that this sweet spot is currently very valuable indeed. At the time of writing, sales figures for the U.S. market alone were 7,866,590 copies sold of *Gone Girl*, 7,460,616 of *The Girl with the Dragon Tattoo*, and 3,731,239 copies of *The Girl on the Train*, which has yet to be released in paperback. These kinds of figures don't happen very often, but the algorithms did reveal some more of the puzzle.

Remember that the novels in our research corpus have a variety of possible shapes. At a very basic level of resolution, we found six or seven fundamental shapes. Some look like a sketched *M*, some like *W*s, some like a slanted *N* or a big *U*. When we studied the basic shapes of all the novels in our corpus, we did not find any one shape that would guarantee market success, but we did find that certain types of books, with certain types of characters, just seem to work. So it meant something to find that the shapes for the big three "girl" novels shared a striking similarity. Our interest in these novels had begun with an almost whimsical conversation about the vogue for girl novels. Was there something to them? The model for character agency had said yes. But the model for plot was the clincher. It showed that the girl novels were not isolated random examples of the dark feminine character done right. They in fact belong together as part of an emerging subgenre. See Figure 16.

These three plotlines are telling. Lisbeth, Amy, and Rachel propel almost identical plotlines and these plotlines deny the traditional ending of satisfying closure. They

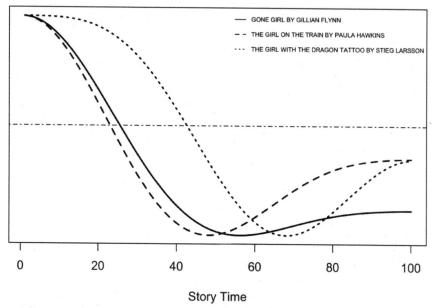

Fig. 16.

show us very clearly that when we get to the end of the book we are not looking at a *Harry Potter* scenario where all is well. The figure of the displaced girl is a part of this, and until authors find this figure her place, "solve her," to put it clearly if crudely, and bring her some resolution, then we think these books will stay in vogue.

What's interesting is both the sharp descent into trouble seen in the first half of these books and then the lack of resolution at the end. It is very clear here that one of the features of this subgenre is a story that ends somewhere less happy than where it began.

The ending strokes of these novels are new and fresh. In *Dragon Tattoo*, Lisbeth recognizes that her relationship to the detective Blomkvist is love and could be relationship. This is very familiar from, oh, hundreds of novels where a man and a woman come together to save the world and then fall in love. So Lisbeth, never passive, takes action and goes to buy Blomkvist a special gift she knows he will appreciate. Will his acceptance of this gift and a relationship with her make this girl a "woman"? Will this be Lisbeth's moment to find her place of belonging? Readers may hope so. But as Lisbeth goes to find the object of her affections, she sees him walking arm in arm in the street with his lover. His lover, by the way, is married to someone else and is in an open relationship. Notably, there is no typical closed and monogamous relationship in this novel: traditional relationships are something all the girl novels toy with. The book ends thus, with Lisbeth dumping the dream of her heart:

"What a pathetic fool you are, Salander," she said out loud.

She turned on her heel and went home to her newly spotless apartment. As she passed Zinkensdamm, it started to snow. She tossed Elvis into a dumpster.

Her apartment is spotless, she is dusted in purifying snow. Her epiphany and the snow are almost Joycean.* Everything is being cleansed. Lisbeth has done her work as agent in cleansing the community but as yet is given no happy place in that community herself.

At the end of *The Girl on the Train*, Rachel does not reunite with her ex-husband as she had originally hoped, and she does

---

* Check out Joyce's short story "The Dead" in *Dubliners*.

not create a relationship with Megan's husband, either, despite their brief tryst. Instead, Rachel realizes that her ex, Tom, is a murderer who has murdered the missing girl, Megan, whom she first saw through the train window. Rachel also realizes that her ex was having an affair with Megan, whose relationship she had idealized from the train carriage, even though he has remarried another different woman. What a mess! It is hardly the satisfying love plot. In self-defense, Rachel kills Tom in front of his new wife with a corkscrew. It's an ironic choice of weapon for an alcoholic. There is something apt about seeing Rachel remove the "dirt" from the system with such an object. Her murderous ex has used Rachel's drinking habit as an alibi, telling her she keeps drunkenly "forgetting" the truth. The corkscrew, once a symbol of a dark girl's failures, becomes the symbol of justice and resolution.

In the very last scene of this book, as with *Dragon Tattoo*, the girl of the title has helped solve a crime, but has not found her own sense of peace or belonging. She is preparing for her next steps, and they are back on the train, alone, again.

> I get into bed and turn the lights out. I won't be able to sleep, but I have to try. Eventually, I suppose, the nightmares will stop and I'll stop replaying it over and over and over in my head, but right now I know that there's a long night ahead. And I have to get up early tomorrow morning to catch the train.

Of the three plot graphs, *Gone Girl*'s suggests the flattest and likely the bleakest ending, and the model is right. By the end of that novel, Amy and Nick are stuck in a twisted marriage full of hidden darkness. Amy has murdered a man, gone back to her husband, bribed and scared him, and has even taken his preserved sperm and had herself impregnated. She has done everything to create the face of the perfect domesticated family, albeit in a dark and blackly ironic mask. The novel ends as she claims the last word, and in doing so traps them both forever. It's a horrific ending, but somehow magnetic.

So, what we see here is inversion of the idealized female, inversion of plotlines, and also inversion of bestselling theme. In the opening chapter, we stated that some of the most success-ful writers know the implied rules of fiction, and know them so well that they beautifully subvert them. The girl novels of-fer a master class in that art. As you may remember, the top theme in indicating a runaway bestseller is human closeness. From reading the plot summaries, it doesn't appear that any of the girl books would have that theme as part of their core DNA. But according to our model, it is in fact the top theme in two of the three, taking 11 percent of *Gone Girl* and 15 percent of *The Girl on the Train*. In both novels, of course, the theme is beautifully distorted in a house of mirrors. Marriage, home, and family become the most alienating of spaces. In *Dragon Tat-too,* closeness is barely a present topic in the thematic makeup at all. It is the forty-seventh most dominant theme, taking less than half a percent of the novel. This absence is palpable throughout the book because it is precisely what she needs— the nearest topic to emotional connection in the top ten topics for Larsson is "interactions with a friend." As readers we want

Lisbeth to realize that despite her brilliance, closeness is what is missing for her. Of course, she does realize this, but she is denied her perfect closure.

These *girl* books are, ultimately, character novels. They give us characters who do not fit or stay in the "all-American girl" role—a role that all three are frustrated with, and that perhaps many readers are frustrated with. There is a sense that what is at stake for these characters and their readers is something deep about the very *herness* of *her* and where she belongs. Lisbeth has been abused and alienated by the system meant to protect her as an orphan. Rachel describes herself as "a barren, divorced, soon-to-be-homeless alcoholic"—an outsider to the traditional feminine roles of mother, wife, homemaker, and then she loses her job too. Amy is always in contrast to Amazing Amy, the namesake character in the bestselling children's series that the real Amy's parents have written. Amazing Amy is a "perfect girl": smart, honest, beautiful, feminine, and good. The pressure she puts on our protagonist Amy is destructive. At the same time, however, Lisbeth is the best hacker in the world, Rachel is an amateur detective, and Amy is a mastermind. They have their special talents, as bestselling characters do, and each is determined to use those talents to find herself a sense of place and belonging. That all three struggle with this in the hands of contemporary writers suggests to us that these fictional girls are doing cultural work that is not yet complete. Until they find their collective closure and peace, we believe they will stay in vogue. A note to our editor: keep buying the girl books.

The Lists: Character

Top ten books for male agency

1. Patricia Cornwell, *Predator*
2. Emily Giffin, *Something Borrowed*
3. Heather Gudenkauf, *The Weight of Silence*
4. E. L. James, *Fifty Shades Darker*
5. Stephen King and Peter Straub, *Black House*
6. Terry McMillan, *How Stella Got Her Groove Back*
7. Erin Morgenstern, *The Night Circus*
8. James Patterson, *Zoo*
9. Jodi Picoult, *My Sister's Keeper*
10. Tom Rachman, *The Imperfectionists*

Top ten books for female agency

1. Patricia Cornwell, *Trace*
2. Emma Donoghue, *Room*
3. Jane Green, *Second Change*
4. John Grisham, *The Racketeer*
5. Sara Gruen, *Water for Elephants*
6. A. S. A. Harrison, *The Silent Wife*
7. E. L. James, *Fifty Shades Freed*
8. Christina Baker Kline, *Orphan Train*
9. James Patterson, *Suzanne's Diary for Nicholas*
10. Jodi Picoult, *House Rules*

6

THE **ONE**, OR, WHEN THE **ALGORITHM** WINKED

When you're at a cocktail party and are introduced to someone new, the first thing this new friend tends to ask you is what you do. If you're like us, then you say that you work with literature. Often the pat response to that answer is "why?"

"Words!" you might say, and when you see that odd, blank stare, you might dig a little deeper. "Sentences, characters, novels, ideas. Stories!"

At this point, you can more or less guarantee the next question. If you're a keen reader and advertise the fact, you likely hear this question as often as we do.

"What is your favorite novel?"

Oh the dread of that question if you are a passionate reader or, worse, a professional one! How to answer it in a way that can satisfy your inquisitive new acquaintance as well as your own panicking, fussy inner voice? Responding, "Oh, my favorite novel changes all the time," is not an acceptable answer. It makes you a flake.

"What is your favorite novel?" is another way of saying, "Tell me the one book I should read." It's a way of saying, "Win me to your cause!" Of course, to a non-book person, say a broker or physician, it's a perfectly legitimate question. Tell me the one stock to buy. Tell me the one health tip that will keep me going. But *one* novel? The pressure!

One way to navigate this call on expertise is to provide a stock answer. If you want to appear erudite you might say *Ulysses*. But then you will likely worry about either alienating your new friend or appearing to be an English major cliché. If you want to appear educated and current, you might pick one of the huge number of half-read but must-read hardcovers on your bedside table. They are possibly written by someone who has an MFA. *Fates and Furies, City on Fire, The Art of Fielding.* The problem then is if you are asked about the ending, you might look like a fool. Another strategy to create the impression of being educated is to pick a popular Pulitzer winner because then you can't go wrong. "Oh, I don't know; this week my favorite might be *The Brief Wondrous Life of Oscar Wao.*" That's a novel full of complicated footnotes, a challenge to explain over a martini, so instead you could pick the beach read you actually had time to get through last time you got a week off. A David Baldacci, a Nora Roberts, a Michael Connelly. But then it seems we are not meant to talk about reading *those* books even though everybody reads them (and, hopefully, after reading this book you'll know why).

What to do? You could just go for a safe choice and say *Life of Pi.* But that feels like a cop-out. Perhaps you've enjoyed many books, and perhaps all your other college favorites start pushing at your tongue, wanting to be spoken. *To Kill a Mockingbird, Pride and Prejudice, The Handmaid's Tale.* Perhaps images from some novels-turned-movies appear in your mind too: at least your new friend might know these plots. *The Road. Silver Linings Playbook. Still Alice.* Finally, you offer a choice and stick with it. You go with *Oscar Wao.* Instantly you know the next inevitable question, another one that is typically answered with some fumbling half-sentences at best.

"Hmm, interesting. Why that book in particular?"

You know, of course, that you can't get away with just saying, "Because it's good." No way.

So let's wait on the answer to that question and look for a moment at what is going on here. Yes, you're at a party trying to explain why Junot Díaz won the Pulitzer Prize. Let us help you out a bit. Díaz's style in *Oscar Wao* is perfect for pleasing a large audience and his characterization, particularly for male characters, is 99 percent ideal. But you're also in a scenario full of unspoken expectations that are endemic to our culture. We have said it before. We live in a culture of *the one.* Selection *matters.* It has implications.

Recommending a book is not like recommending a health tip or a stock. Recommending a book can be like trying to navigate the unspoken rules and faux pas of a Jane Austen ballroom. The book world comes with considerable baggage. Snobbery is rife, and so is reverse snobbery. Taste is on the line. So is class. So are more stigmas and stereotypes than anyone would want to be associated with. The stigma of the erotica reader.

The stereotype of the science fiction reader. The distaste for the elitist advocate of whatever "real literature" is. All of this sits unspoken in the choice of the favorite book that you share with your new friend, and this is precisely why naming and explaining it can be like offering a stranger a hidden part of your soul. All this baggage sits unspoken in the manifestation of every list of chosen books we publish as a culture too. Book talk can be very volatile. It's not just the bestseller lists, and all the opinions that exist (unqualified, mostly) about them that stir emotions. Look at what happened in 2001 when Oprah Winfrey recommended Jonathan Franzen's *The Corrections*. He infamously called her other selections "schmaltzy" and said his work was too highbrow to appear in her book club. Look at what happened in 1960 when Penguin Books recommended *Lady Chatterley's Lover*. There was a high-profile court case against the publisher because of its racy content. Look at what happened when Mark Zuckerberg shared his recommended reading list. Major newspapers all over the world printed it with their commentary. This commentary can be most easily summarized with reference to the English newspaper that invited readers to look at the list and what it supposedly said about the Facebook CEO. Exactly what his choices said about him was left unspoken, apparently quite obvious. There is always press, opinion, and controversy when someone recommends a book publically. Always.

Back at the party.

Everyone is talking about their favorite book and why. Someone might say *"The Orphan Master's Son* because Adam Johnson is awesome."* Certainly, that is true. Another person

could say *"The Fault in Our Stars* because I cried my eyes out."
People would sympathize. But what if you could bring something
new to this old conversation. Perhaps it is compelling. Perhaps it is outrageous. But surely it is of the moment.

What would happen if you said you were going to bypass
the messy terrain of taste with all its land mines and instead
you were going to name the favorite book of an algorithm?
What would happen if you said this algorithm had read thousands of books and, without being trained to do so, gave
one novel, just that all-important *one,* a score of the perfect
100 percent? And what if it could explain its choice not just with
the odd word or two, but with pages of spreadsheets and graphs?
What, we wonder, would your new friend with his cocktail
make of the choice, and why? Would you be able to stand by
the algorithm's choice, even as a "book person"?

These were the questions we faced before we committed
to this project. They were risky. But part of what was new for
us was the blind faith we decided to put into our model. We'd
share its results, whatever they were. What we didn't know at
that time was that it would join in the fun of picking just one,
and that the choice, when it was finally given after five years
of training, would be so uncanny.

So—be it utopian, dystopian, or just outright nerdish—we
invite the computer to the cocktail party.

Sweet Spot

At this point, you have learned what we do, and you should
have a pretty good idea about the basics of the bestseller-ometer.

In the opening chapter, we explained that the model takes thousands of points of data to create an aggregate score for a likely appearance on the *New York Times* bestseller list. In our corpus, the yes and no scores have proven to be right about 80 percent of the time. Every book also receives a score estimating just how likely it is to be a bestseller. Most of the novels we have discussed in this book got scores above 90 percent. In chapter 2, we looked at just the part of the algorithm that identifies topics in fiction, as well as which topics in which proportions tend to sell and keep selling. The machine showed us that the books that do best in the market have three or four central themes that occupy about 30 percent of the pages. Many other themes, in smaller proportions, add flavor. The computer revealed that the most frequently occurring and important theme is one that involves human closeness, a theme that is all about characters relating emotionally. Some of the other top themes included the home, work (the topic Stephen King says people always want to read about), kids in school, and modern technologies.

In chapter 3 we looked at plotlines, which were effectively modeled by tracking the use of emotional language. Though bestsellers can take many shapes, a remarkably high number of the biggest hits from the last thirty years share a plot shape with a regular beating rhythm. The model showed that symmetry in a plotline, and a clear three-act structure, tend to indicate that readers will find a novel pleasing, and we also saw that a carefully manipulated emotional ride can lead to high global sales.

But without an understanding of style, no author will make it to the list, even with the right themes and a driving plotline. In chapter 4, we showed how the model analyzes style as part of its overall guess. When it comes to bestselling style, we found that an understanding of everyday language was essential. If you want to master winning style, a training in literature is not a bad idea but some added practical experience working in journalism, or advertising, or marketing is probably a very good idea.

Chapter 5 explained the close relationship between bestselling characters and the verbs used to described their actions. We described the current vogue for the dark or misplaced feminine and the sort of plotline she creates. This female character tends to lead stories that threaten the sanctity of the domestic sphere, bringing some of the horrors of the public and global sphere into the most intimate spaces in a character's life. Her agency is powerful, and somewhat frightening.

We must admit that we love the idea that there may be a novelist out there reading these words, thinking: "Oh my. I wrote 'The One.'" We wonder if this author, who must have a deep instinct for the current pulse of the age, is so savvy that he or she knows what a computer knows. Which is that he or she aced what it takes to best sell. Can anyone be so aware during the creative process?

While each of the chapters has taken a different element of fiction, it is a somewhat misleading approach. We can learn a lot about how novels work by looking at their themes, or their style, but the truth is that the effect of fiction is created by the interdependencies between all these different elements. One aspect cannot be written without the others. The wrong character creates the wrong plotline. The wrong set of themes limits the kind of character that can walk onto the page. To achieve big success, an author really has to stand out in every aspect of fiction that we have discussed. For a high score from our model, an author has to have achieved a hidden sweet spot in every aspect of novel writing, from the title and the first line to the last paragraph and all the emotional terrain in between.

Anatomy of a Perfect Story

As you know, the model we created gives us graphs and tables for every book. Every manuscript has its own report of about fifteen pages—telling us everything from the overarching plotline to the use of the word "the," the verbs that go with different characters, and the frequency of adjectives such as "little," "important," and "black." After reading several hundred of these reports and watching the performance of the published manuscripts, you learn to recognize an exciting report when it comes off the printer.

We got one book report—one—that looked like this.

1) Topical makeup.
Three themes make up roughly 30 percent, which we know to be a winning formula. The DNA is 21 percent Modern Technology, 4 percent Jobs and the Workplace, and 3 percent

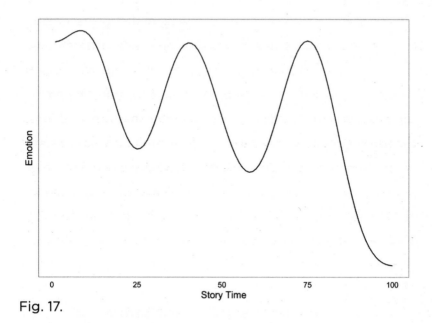

Fig. 17.

Human Closeness. There's our top theme in the top three, and the other two themes are both top ten.

2) Plot.

The three-act plotline is the same as *Fifty Shades of Grey*. The emotional plotline, which gives more scene-by-scene detail, has a symmetry reserved for a small percentage of published novels. The plotline ends in a darker place than where it began. In that, it shares characteristics with not only *Fifty Shades of Grey* but the novels that constitute the "girl book" phenomenon. See Figure 17.

3) Stylistic analysis.

The style is almost perfectly balanced between the "masculine" style of traditionally educated prize winners, and the "feminine" style of writers with a background in journalism, advertising, and the media. The style split is 52 percent "feminine," and 48 percent "masculine." Incidence of contractions such as "-'ll" and "-d" is in line with bestsellers, as are the other subtle aspects of style that create voice. Exclamation marks are appropriately low, whereas commas and period points are high enough to indicate sentences of the right length.

4) Character.
The novel's female characters are 99.9 percent likely to bestsell. The protagonist is female. She has great agency and is central to a plotline that ends in a darker place than where it began. Her most-used verbs are *need* and *want*.

5) Overall confidence that this book belongs in the *NYT* bestseller club.
100 percent.
The whole book report was like cocaine to two book-world nerds.

And did this manuscript hit the lists? Yes. Did we, as professors of literature and keen readers, think it was a good choice? Well to be honest, we didn't know. We hadn't read it. But the author surprised and intrigued us, and so did the title. We had figured the winner would likely be a novel by a veteran author who had clearly mastered and repeated the fundamentals of bestselling over and over again. Perhaps a Lee Child, or a Nora Roberts, or a John Grisham. We had made some friendly bets on Nicholas Sparks and Janet Evanovich.

We also thought that perhaps the machine would pick a non-genre writer—someone who understands the rules and expectations of different genres but inverts or breaks them well. Matt kept making a case for Emma Donoghue's novel *Room* and Jodie had insisted he read *The Lovely Bones* by Alice Sebold. We had a lot of fun campaigning with each other for the various commercial merits of different writers. But still, neither of us had considered the novel that came out on top.

The model's favorite manuscript of the past thirty years was *The Circle* by Dave Eggers.

Stranger than Fiction

Dave Eggers would do very well as a character in a novel. His biography has many of the ingredients of a fictional male hero in an archetypal plot. Perhaps, like a good bestselling character, he has the self-awareness to know that. Eggers actually rose to literary fame writing about himself. His breakout book, *A Heartbreaking Work of Staggering Genius* (now *that* was a title) was a memoir about raising his younger brother in California after the death of both their parents. Eggers was what we have called a debutant—his first book hit the lists. Actually, the memoir reached number one on the *NYT* lists *and* was a finalist for a Pulitzer Prize. It's a rare writer who instinctively understands the audience so fully; not only the mass readership involved in charting with a debut, but also the tastes of prestigious prize committees. That kind of instant positioning in the market is in part about a strong sense of style.

In this book, we have talked about authorial style in simple terms as a mixture of nature and nurture. Algorithms have shown us not only that every writer has an innate stylistic fingerprint, but that computers can often recognize major and formative influences on a writer, especially the difference between a traditional literary education and journalistic training. Many authors who debut onto the lists have a journalistic background, and Eggers is no different. He has a degree in journalism and started a publishing house as well as a journal, *Timothy McSweeney's Quarterly Concern,* before his first book was published. But Eggers, unlike most of his fellow novelists with journalistic backgrounds, does not write with the dominantly "feminine" style we discussed in chapter 4. His sentences are almost exactly 50/50, meaning he has captured the style most typical to bestsellers *and* the style most likely to be recognized by prize-giving institutions. Eggers has won, among other prizes, the American Book Award, the Northern California Book Award, the Dayton Literary Peace Prize, the Prix Médicis, the Heinz Award, and a TED Prize. His list of accolades includes *Time* Best Book of the Year, *Washington Post* Best Book of the Year, an honorary Doctor of Letters from Brown University, and nominations for many other literary prizes.

But it turns out Eggers is not just a smart writer at the center of a personal adversity-to-triumph plot. He's also, like the popular fictional male, somewhat of a superhero. Eggers is the cofounder of a nonprofit writing and tutoring center for kids, and he launched a second nonprofit organization that matches low-income youths with donors to enable them to go to college. He has written many works of fiction and nonfiction, one about the injustice experienced by a man named Zeitoun after Hurricane Katrina, and another—a novel—based on the true story of a Sudanese refugee. He is married with two children. He is commonly thought of as a handsome man.

Having been focused for so long on stories that sell, it is hard to look at his life choices (his character agency, so to speak), and not see bestselling themes and emotional data all over them. On paper at least, Eggers is basically a walking idealized American male, the example of the perfect male lead that we were lacking in the last chapter on the "girls." Was this guy for real? Was he in cahoots with our computer?

Oh, the model had more fun with us than that.

Neither one of us had read *The Circle* when the bestsellerometer flagged it as perfect for the lists. We felt like fools. Of course, we immediately bought copies and read the book rapidly and in tandem, a frequent phone call away. Our reading started out quite gleeful. Naturally, we were trying to understand its latent DNA, its anatomical brilliance. The title, of course, is one of the "The" titles, and its noun is abstract, pregnant. What is a circle? Something complete, something suggesting community perhaps, something that carries a touch of mysticism. What is *the* circle? Who knew, but we were about to find out.

The point so far was that the title works, and so does the first sentence of the book. It is exactly on target. "My God, Mae thought, it's heaven." The line has all the ingredients of bestselling that we have discussed in the past four chapters. Grammatical balance. Brevity. Contractions. Tone. A female

protagonist doing a bestselling verb. But also a female protagonist who, in referring so rapidly in a novel to heaven may or
may not be about to walk right into hell. Is she, we wondered,
one of "those girls"?

We have written about many opening lines of bestselling
novels. Often, their work is an emotional setup. The openings
that work give us a relationship between the first character we
meet and someone or something else around them, present or
implied. That relationship is often going to give us a central
conflict. In the examples we gave in chapter 4, this other person
has been an irritating cop, a lover, a family member perhaps.
Mae trumps that. In fact, Mae trumps many literary protagonists in lots of ways. The first relationship she evokes is not
with any fellow mortal, but with the divine. Mae, unless she is
dead, thinks she has found heaven on earth. It's a prescient
and ironic opening to a novel that, we find out, has a clever
relationship to omniscience and utopia. The foreboding we
may feel from that first line is not misplaced—look at the plotline and how soon after the initial euphoria we are going to
see Mae walk right into a steep emotional ditch.

Mae walks into her heaven on earth when she starts a new
job. Her employer is in fact a futuristic tech company that looks
a lot like what would happen if Google and Facebook had an
illegitimate love child and then dressed it in Apple hardware.
This scenario is established in the opening pages and explains
the novel's thematic DNA: 21 percent Modern Technology,
4 percent Jobs and the Workplace, and 3 percent Human Closeness. Much of the novel's subtext is about what the influence
of the first two of these themes might be on the third. Therein

lies what we explained in chapter 2, namely the likely conflict generated by the top few themes of the novel. The book report told us even before we had started reading that this was likely another one of those bestselling novels that keeps closeness as a central theme but subverts it.

Part of Mae's first job at the Circle is to keep improving a formulaic written document—a sort of customer response slip—in order to improve customer satisfaction. Her success at work is measured by surveys that give her a percentage score. A score of 98 is passable but not ideal. A score of 93 is terrible. The perfect 100 is the holy grail. To achieve it, Mae has to understand her audience and tweak the perfect written formula to suit their interests and satisfy them intellectually and emotionally. Yes, we are aware of the irony. Our algorithm seemed to have somehow picked itself.

As we both dove deep into the story of Mae at the Circle, we recognized many current bestselling moves at play. Mae is not just the dark feminine, but the dark feminine at her zenith. She does not, like the "girls" who have recently hit the lists, just bring something threatening and potentially horrific into the private spaces of home, relationship, and family. She is actually the face of the total eradication of public and private space. She eliminates all boundaries, and does so with a smile. Thanks to her willingness to be the spokeswoman for the Circle's latest products, Mae uses her character agency in the name of modern technology's total invasion of not just the home and relationships but also the psyche. And Mae, also unlike the other girls on the *NYT* lists, either lacks or suppresses the self-awareness to prevent disaster and recognize her role in failed relationships. The novel ends not with a sense of learning and new direction but with her call to allow technology to read her best friend's thoughts. "Why shouldn't they know them?" she thinks. "The world deserved nothing less and will not wait." While it starts in "heaven," Eggers' plot certainly ends in a nightmarish vision of a potential technological dystopia, like one of Dante's circles of hell.

We don't want to say a lot more about the book. It warrants a read, and there are too many potential spoilers. Suffice to say that when we read Eggers' novel we found further faith in our algorithm—the book demonstrates the sweet spot of the different aspects of bestselling fiction and in their own unique combination. But we also found ourselves feeling that something more than a little uncanny was going on.

It's a little awkward. Dave Eggers wrote a novel full of warning about new and advanced technologies, in which his protagonist is measured by percentage points. She is one of the stars at her job, pushing closer and closer toward 100 percent, which will bring her recognition not just from customers but from her peers. What can we say? Dave Eggers, you got 100 percent. Whether you knew it or not, and whether you like it or not, you tweaked the hidden formulas of fiction, even down to the use of commas and conjunctions and everyday nouns. According to the computer, you are the paradigmatic writer of the past thirty years. The algorithm appears to have winked at us all. We weren't sure whether we should take a sledgehammer to it, or buy it dinner.

Honorable Mentions

If we took our model to a cocktail party, it would likely be a provocative guest. We knew that as soon as we started this project. But the smarter it became, the more it seemed to grow awareness (untrained, we should add), of precisely the right and wrong things to say. After it told us that its top recommendation of all books in a generation of publishing was one in which advanced computing is portrayed as the likely collapse of ethical and civilized humanity, we asked it to give us its top pick of all writers that the market considers to be literary.

Its answer? Jonathan Franzen. *Freedom,* it said, is its favorite literary novel. Oh dear. Was it not aware of the furor when Oprah Winfrey picked Jonathan Franzen, never mind a computer? Did it not know about the column inches that followed Oprah's choice, about the fight between the highbrow and the lowbrow, the elite and the masses, good and bad writing, and whose business it is and is not to comment on such matters? It didn't care. It gave him a solid 90 percent and put him on a list right next to Sylvia Day. The two writers are not, it turns out, as fundamentally dissimilar as both may like to think.

We asked it about the public spat between James Patterson and Stephen King. King is famous for swiping at Patterson about his inability to write. Patterson is famous for referring, in response to such criticisms, to his massive sales. Which, we asked, is the author who better demonstrates bestseller list writing?

In this case, there was no dramatic response. They can both

do it, said the model. They will keep doing it too. But, when pushed, the nod went to Patterson.

We hope the bestseller-ometer is trained to recognize what readers want. We hope it understands what fiction is for millions of people who give their leisure time to stories that are well put together. When it comes to the factions of fiction, the model seems to be a great equalizer. It will champion authors all over the market.

Which was its second favorite novel, after Eggers? Jodi Picoult's *House Rules*. It gave high points to all of her work, but its top two were *House Rules* and *Nineteen Minutes*. After Picoult, it favored another novel neither of us had read, but another we were happy to have recommended. Maria Semple's *Where'd You Go, Bernadette,* it showed us, is an almost ideal example of all the ingredients readers keep buying.

In the end, we were unable to resist some list making of our own. At the end of this chapter is the computer's ranked recommended reading list—one hundred novels that we hope will have something for everyone.

Researching this book has fundamentally changed our attitudes toward literature, writing, and literary criticism. It has developed us as readers and teachers, and has introduced us to some of our favorite living authors. When Jodie went to Matt in 2010 and said she wanted to give bestsellers some serious attention, he admits his first reaction was "Huh?" He had been working on a tool that would detect the signal of great works of literature—"the canonizer" as he had dubbed it—and she wanted to study the books you buy at the airport during a layover. He was, after all, trained as a Joycean. He taught *Ulysses*.

He had read every page of *Finnegans Wake* and could recite the first and last from memory, which he did, incidentally, at departmental cocktail parties.

Jodie, on the other hand, was once the voice in Matt's digital humanities classroom who said, "So what?" With a background in publishing and contemporary literature, she simply didn't see the point of the presence of the computer in literary scholarship. When she was told a computer knew if a Shakespeare play was a tragedy or a comedy she said: "Who cares?" Human researchers already knew all this. She was defensive of the traditional methods for publishing, analyzing, and recommending books. Well, Matt took what he smilingly called her "attitude problem" as a challenge and kept coding. Now she is just about ready to start a computational book club.

These days the cocktail parties and Matt's classes are a lot different. Matt's become quite a fan of *The Devil Wears Prada,* and it only takes a few drinks to get him to tell you all about *Fifty Shades of Grey.* And if you listen carefully at that same cocktail party, you can sometimes hear Jodie using phrases like "latent Dirichlet allocation" with admirable efficiency. Though he still taught his standard *Ulysses* seminar this year, he also added a new class on contemporary bestsellers that we picked together. Students read Dan Brown, Anthony Doerr, Gillian Flynn, John Grisham, Sue Monk Kidd, Alice Sebold, and Nicholas Sparks. We taught two of these classes together and came to see just how important it is that students of literature are exposed to these most successful living writers.

We think the bestseller-ometer has the potential to change how we write, publish, and read new fiction. We hope it has brought some respect to those mainstream novelists who are often dismissed. We hope it will inspire new authors. And we hope it has given even the most stalwart traditionalist something fresh. Ultimately, the bestseller-ometer is one manifestation of a new way to approach literature, and at the same time a new tool to help us see and appreciate just how wonderful a good book can be.

The Lists: All Data Points

100 novels our computer thinks you should read

1. Dave Eggers, *The Circle*
2. Jodi Picoult, *House Rules*
3. Maria Semple, *Where'd You Go, Bernadette*
4. Michael Connelly, *The Burning Room*
5. David Baldacci, *The Hit*
6. Patricia Cornwell, *Scarpetta*
7. Harlan Coben, *Six Years*
8. James Patterson, *Double Cross*
9. Janet Evanovich, *Twelve Sharp*
10. William Landay, *Defending Jacob*
11. Tom Rachman, *The Imperfectionists*
12. Jessica Knoll, *Luckiest Girl Alive*
13. Matthew Quick, *The Silver Linings Playbook*
14. Wally Lamb, *The Hour I First Believed*
15. Graeme Simsion, *The Rosie Project*

16. Lisa Scottoline, *Look Again*
17. Tom Clancy, *Dead or Alive*
18. Liane Moriarty, *The Husband's Secret*
19. Tim LaHaye and Jerry Jenkins, *The Mark*
20. Jennifer Weiner, *Best Friends Forever*
21. Emily Giffin, *Heart of the Matter*
22. Lisa Genova, *Still Alice*
23. Mitch Albom, *The First Phone Call from Heaven*
24. Gillian Flynn, *Gone Girl*
25. Jonathan Tropper, *This Is Where I Leave You*
26. Nelson DeMille, *Wild Fire*
27. Kate Jacobs, *The Friday Night Knitting Club*
28. Stephen King, *Cell*
29. Barbara Kingsolver, *Flight Behavior*
30. Jonathan Franzen, *Freedom*
31. Dan Brown, *The Lost Symbol*
32. Chris Culver, *The Abbey*
33. Jane Green, *Second Chance*
34. Vince Flynn, *The Last Man*
35. John Grisham, *The Associate*
36. Chimamanda Ngozi Adichie, *Americanah*
37. Emma McLaughlin and Nicola Kraus, *The Nanny Diaries*
38. Lauren Weisberger, *The Devil Wears Prada*
39. Michael Crichton, *Next*
40. Sylvia Day, *Entwined with You*
41. Kristin Hannah, *Firefly Lane*

42. Lee Child, *Personal*
43. Tatiana de Rosnay, *A Secret Kept*
44. Jacquelyn Mitchard, *The Deep End of the Ocean*
45. Paula Hawkins, *The Girl on the Train*
46. Emma Donoghue, *Room*
47. J. Courtney Sullivan, *Maine*
48. Raymond Khoury, *The Last Templar*
49. J. K. Rowling, *The Casual Vacancy*
50. Andy Weir, *The Martian*
51. Chad Harbach, *The Art of Fielding*
52. Jonathan Safran Foer, *Extremely Loud and Incredibly Close*
53. Jamie McGuire, *Beautiful Disaster*
54. Anita Shreve, *Testimony*
55. Jennifer Egan, *A Visit from the Goon Squad*
56. Curtis Sittenfeld, *American Wife*
57. E. L. James, *Fifty Shades of Grey*
58. Jan Karon, *Somewhere Safe with Somebody Good*
59. Nora Roberts, *The Next Always*
60. Tana French, *In the Woods*
61. Nicholas Sparks, *The Choice*
62. Jojo Moyes, *Me Before You*
63. Julian Barnes, *The Sense of an Ending*
64. Jess Walter, *Beautiful Ruins*
65. Christina Baker Kline, *Orphan Train*
66. Alice Sebold, *The Lovely Bones*
67. Dean Koontz, *The Darkest Evening of the Year*

68. Wm. Paul Young, *Cross Roads*
69. Donna Tartt, *The Goldfinch*
70. Junot Díaz, *The Brief Wondrous Life of Oscar Wao*
71. Eric Van Lustbader, *The Bourne Betrayal*
72. Jennifer Probst, *The Marriage Bargain*
73. Heather Gudenkauf, *The Weight of Silence*
74. Terry McMillan, *A Day Late and a Dollar Short*
75. Aravind Adiga, *The White Tiger*
76. Robert Galbraith, *The Cuckoo's Calling*
77. Khaled Hosseini, *And the Mountains Echoed*
78. David Sedaris, *Squirrel Seeks Chipmunk*
79. Mary Higgins Clark, *Daddy's Gone a Hunting*
80. Charlaine Harris, *Dead in the Family*
81. Garth Stein, *The Art of Racing in the Rain*
82. A. S. A. Harrison, *The Silent Wife*
83. Jamie Ford, *Hotel on the Corner of Bitter and Sweet*
84. Anne Tyler, *A Spool of Blue Thread*
85. Danielle Steel, *The Klone and I*
86. John Sandford, *Easy Prey*
87. Max Brooks, *World War Z*
88. Eleanor Brown, *The Weird Sisters*
89. Jhumpa Lahiri, *Unaccustomed Earth*
90. Adam Johnson, *The Orphan Master's Son*
91. Nicholas Evans, *The Horse Whisperer*
92. David Nicholls, *One Day*
93. Elizabeth Strout, *Olive Kitteridge*

94. Stieg Larsson, *The Girl Who Kicked the Hornets' Nest*
95. Darcie Chan, *The Mill River Recluse*
96. John Hart, *The Last Child*
97. Chris Cleave, *Little Bee*
98. Joe Klein, *Primary Colors*
99. Ann Patchett, *State of Wonder*
100. Dennis Lehane, *Shutter Island*

Epilogue

THE MACHINE-WRITTEN NOVEL, OR, WHY AUTHORS REALLY MATTER

So, a whole book about computers reading, but what about the next logical question: Can computers write?

In November 2013, Darius Kazemi tweeted a crazy idea. The tweet read: "Hey, who wants to join me in NaNoGenMo: spend the month writing code that generates a 50k word novel, share the novel & the code at the end."

NaNoGenMo is National Novel Generation Month, an invention of Kazemi. He is a self-described "Internet artist" who is best known for writing computer programs, or "bots," that use existing text (from social media and other electronic sources) to algorithmically produce new expressions. One of Kazemi's bots randomly generates awkward pickup lines: "Girl, you must be a melamine because you are a plastic made from such resin." "Boy, you must be a megabyte because you are a unit of computer memory or data storage capacity equal to 1,048,576 (220) bytes." Another of Kazemi's programs generates a "metaphor a minute." The confusing one-liners pumped out of this bot read more like Zen bumper stickers than elegant figures of speech. On January 4, 2016, the @metaphorminute bot on Twitter cranked out such prize-winners as: "a marmot is a piste: coxcombly and decrepid [*sic*]" and the slightly more interesting and deeper musing that "a biographer is a rubberneck: ill-bred, and surveyable." The vast majority of these bot-generated lines are absurd, lacking both in sense and human depth. Still, on occasion, you bump into a particularly provocative bot tweet that is just a little too profound, and you can't help wondering, if only for a moment, about just how winking and sly these machine minds are becoming.

Kazemi's mission in creating his bots seems to be two parts having fun and one part subversive critique. His art inspires both chuckling and apprehension. The work has a certain cleverness. It makes us wonder and giggle in delightful ways about those quirky machines and that rascally Turing test in which machines win when they trick us into thinking they are us.

Kazemi's more ambitious tweet about machines generating entire novels got a lot of press. It was inspired by National Novel Writing Month, or NaNoWriMo, an annual writing challenge sponsored and organized by a 501(c)(3) nonprofit organization that promotes "writing fluency, creative education, and the sheer joy of novel-writing." NaNoWriMo invites people to spend a month writing a 50,000-word novel; Kazemi invited his followers on Twitter to spend a month training a computer to do the actual writing.

This idea was not entirely new. Back in 1952, British computer scientist Christopher Strachey followed his work on the

first computational game of checkers and the first music program to play nursery rhymes with an effort to get computers
to write love letters. His code, which worked on a machine he
learned about through Alan Turing called the Ferranti Mark 1,
"wrote" by pulling random salutations, nouns, verbs, and other
parts of speech from a preprogrammed list and dropping them
into various grammatical constructions. The amorous notes it
turned out were fairly short, quickly to the point. The program
is still available online. The letter it wrote us, all in its moment's
Courier font and capital letters, reads as follows.

```
HONEY DUCK,
   MY  PRECIOUS  LOVE  SEDUCTIVELY  PANTS
FOR  YOUR  CRAVING.  MY  ENCHANTMENT  BURN-
INGLY  WOOS  YOUR  PRECIOUS  PASSION.  YOU
ARE MY PRECIOUS FELLOW FEELING, MY BREATH-
LESS FERVOUR, MY BURNING FERVOUR.
                    YOURS IMPATIENTLY,


                              M.U.C.
```

A seduction from another time! We can't imagine Sylvia
Day—our current-day doyenne of penned passion—feeling all
that threatened by this enigmatic figure M.U.C. (which, by the
way, stands for Manchester University Computer). But that
wasn't really the point of the experiment. The Mark 1 that
created it, which was the first commercially available general purpose computer, was more regularly used for complex
mathematics. Strachey's love letters were not so much either a

genuine effort at Shakespeare, or work in the name of sheer whimsy and amusement, but were instead an attempt to investigate whether or not computers may be capable of sentient thought and emotional expression. It is the investigation into the limits of artificial intelligence (AI) that makes the idea of computers writing novels interesting.

When he became Google's director of engineering, AI developer Ray Kurzweil predicted that computers would outsmart all humans, even the smart ones, by 2029. For that prediction to come true, machines will have to achieve not just intellectual reasoning but emotional and creative expression. Part of that, of course, is writing.

Most people are surprised to hear that some of the sports and business reporting they read in the news could well be computer generated. Kris Hammon, chief scientist and cofounder of a company called Narrative Science, claims that his team is now "humanizing the machine and . . . giving it the tools to know how to tell us stories." He says that "Narrative Science's computers provide daily market reports for *Forbes* as well as sports reports for the Big Ten sports network. Automated Insights [another company] does all the data-based stock reports for AP [Associated Press]." Hammond even claims that his machines have mastered the art of spin and can bias stories to better suit particular audiences.

But writing novels, surely, is something else. There is still, in our opinion, a real and important gulf between computer-generation of text and what could legitimately be called computational creative writing. It won't be fair to claim that a computer has achieved the latter until a computer has cracked a bestselling original love story.

Why?

Well, there is something about taking love as a topic for a computer writing that strikes most people as quite different from a machine producing a quick and factual news broadcast. Human love—or, even more accurately, the topic we labeled as most important to bestselling in chapter 2, which was human closeness—is the topic that is most tantalizing in the debate about the relationship between man and machine. This is likely why Strachey chose love letters as his genre in 1952. Many people will remember Philip K. Dick's 1968 short novel *Do Androids Dream of Electric Sheep?* as its 1982 filmic reinterpretation *Blade Runner*. The story has become a cult classic, not least because its characters are both humans and cyborgs. How will they interact? Can the humanized robot ever really pass as human? In that story, the cyborgs are eerily able to perform human tasks, but they stop short of being able to perform humanity. The ultimate difference between the natural and the coded person in Dick's science fiction narrative is empathy, and so while the novel threatens the collapse of boundaries between man and machine, it is usually interpreted as a reaffirmation of humans as emotionally and spiritually complex beings who could never be part of a factory line. The highest emotion of love, in its expression as compassion and empathy, is humanity's secret sauce.

The 2013 Spike Jonze movie *Her* took this idea up again. In that story, the protagonist, Theodore, writes intimate letters on behalf of other people and falls in love with his new computer operating system, Samantha, who is advanced enough to imitate the expressions of a loving human relationship. The appeal of the plot is that possibility dramatized. The love affair ends, however, when the computer in the relationship decides to dump her intimacy with Theodore in order to continue exploring her existence and accelerated learning capabilities in other dimensions of time.

The point of this breakup, perhaps, is not unlike the implication of Dave Eggers' novel *The Circle*. The moral we seem to be offered is that computers will go the way of being further and further developed for their own sake—deep human relationships are sacrificed on that silicon altar. But for Theodore, who struggles with the callousness of his computer girlfriend, the ending of his e-affair is a return to his own authentic creativity. He is shown for the first time writing an emotional letter not for someone else for work, but in his own name to his ex-wife. We might take both from *Her* and Philip K. Dick's story a defense of the core difference between what makes humans and machines.

Human closeness, then, is as much of an attractive topic for experiments in AI and computer writing as it is for the bestseller list, but the topic also shows the experiments' flaws. The very first commonly recognized novel written by algorithms was called *True Love.wrt*. This was in 2008, before Kazemi called for a mass effort via Twitter. The programmers of this new type of novel were Russian, and this likely explains why all of the characters have the same names as characters from Tolstoy's *Anna Karenina*. That classic tragic love story was uploaded alongside seventeen modern Russian novels and one Japanese novel in translation. The lines of bestselling literary author Haruki Murakami were taken as the style guide for the prototype and inform the cadences of *True Love.wrt*.

The silent influence of Tolstoy and Murakami made for some passable sentences. Description looks like this:

> "The setting sun was painting pink the underbellies of the clouds hanging low above the grey sea. White caps could be seen here and there, but it was obvious that the storm he had been expecting all day was not going to happen."

Representation of a character's inner mind reads like this:

> "Kitty couldn't fall asleep for a long time. Her nerves were strained as two tight strings, and even a glass of hot wine, that Vronsky made her drink, did not help her. Lying in bed she kept going over and over that monstrous scene at the meadow."

Many editors would likely cringe at the tight string metaphor, but we have read worse ones from human writers. What is compelling is the fact that the machine offered a metaphor in the first place, and that the adjectives that precede nouns are actually fitting. In the M.U.C. poem "precious fellow feeling" was laughable, but "hot wine" works, as does "monstrous scene." There is a definite improvement. To read the novel, though, is not an edge-of-seat experience. All the characters speak in the same way, in the same sorts of sentences. Representation of individualized consciousness is very hard to achieve with code.

In Russia, the novel was published to be a sensation, as something groundbreaking and vastly new. Reviews joked that finally commissioning editors would not have to deal with writers not being on time, or with book contracts having to be renegotiated because of an unexpected pregnancy or too much drinking. But reviewers of the work itself were less sure. What must be realized, in fairness, is that the improvement between the love letters and the lines from the novel had a lot more to do with the quality of the writers being cribbed than it had to do with great strides being made toward computers having creative and emotional intelligence. The computer novel like this can only ever be a forgery. There are more and less clever forgeries, and more and less entertaining mash-ups, but forgery is not creation, and recycling is not really creation, either.

Kazemi's "Content, Forever" program allows users to enter a starting, "seed" topic (such as love, or death). The program then looks up this word in Wikipedia and grabs some of the text from the first few paragraphs. The machine then identifies links to other articles in those paragraphs and follows those links. From those Web pages, it takes more text and puts them together in a sort of stream-of-machine-consciousness creation.

The avant-garde Dadaists were up to this in the 1920s, and the technique that became known as the cut-up technique was made more popular by the Beat generation novelist William S. Burroughs in the 1950s. The name came from the simplicity of the method. Newspapers and other printed literature were printed, cut into individual words and phrases, and rearranged for new effect, often without much care for meaning or flow. The juxtapositions of strange words created their own proxies for literary meaning and effect. The method has now been played with in film, recorded speech, and music. David Bowie, Michael Stipe, and Thom Yorke of Radiohead have all made lyrics from cut-ups.

So it is hard to claim that there is much originality either of idea or expression in the enterprise of writing code that will create some version of a cut-up novel. It is also difficult to believe these novels will be very absorbing either mentally or emotionally. Novelists are trained to write what they know, and to rely on their own consciousness full of lived experience for ideas. If the creative's source of "what they know" is Wikipedia, then while some nonfiction reference books seem possible, the computer will remain stumped at creating enthralling fiction, which is about the inwardly spiritual as well as the outwardly factual experiences of human beings.

World Clock, a computer-generated novel, was Nick Monfort's contribution to NaNoGenMo in 2013, and it has the distinction of having been generated with just 165 lines of Python code and then published by the Harvard Book Store. Like other examples, the code and the paragraphs it created reveal what is essentially a sentence and paragraph assembly factory capable of punching out the same set of three- or four-sentence widgets in a variety of different flavors. Every paragraph has three sentences; every first sentence begins with the words "It is"; every second sentence with "In some"; and every third with either the male pronoun "He" or the female pronoun "She." This likely will not be storytelling to rival any author we have discussed in this book, or any of the runners-up. The formal expression is about as exciting as the most wooden five-paragraph high school essay. Yet few people would claim they would choose to read a book like *World Clock* for its story-telling.

So what is this phenomenon about? Ultimately, the attraction of *World Clock* and its contemporaries is the fact that a machine wrote it. Our cultural interest in these projects at the moment is much more to do with novelty and amusement than the future of fiction. Computer-writing is fun because of the absurd ironies it randomly produces. If we were to take from its stories any abstract meaning or truth, it might be something about the lack of sincerity and meaning in a technologically oversaturated world. While that message has a certain appeal for some, we caution giving the machine-written novel too much esteem. Within that technologically oversaturated culture, the novelist's job is not absurdism, but rather the business of creating and unveiling what is meaningful in a hectic world. That is part of the art form. If computers are supposedly becoming smarter than humans, then those smarts are to be measured in terms of accumulated facts and data and rote memorization. But these are skills of the "book smart" person, not the novelist, whose skill is that she is a creative and critical thinker. Computer writing as an alternative to traditional novel writing is quirky and enjoyable only in snippets, and its likely ideal form is there—in snippets to make us chuckle.

Given our research on novels using algorithms, we are often asked about our interest in a machine producing a novel. It is natural to wonder what programmers might be able to do if given access to all of the data that we have compiled for our work on bestsellers. We trained our computers to detect and measure the presence of several thousand ingredients that are essential to bestselling. It might be an attractive idea to take all this data and develop new scripts that build novels from our set of variables.

Such a novel might be more likely to appeal to the public than some of the other computer-created stories out there, but it is not something we have interest in. That is because the opportunity comes from pulling strongly either from the work of real novelists (as with *True Love.wrt*) or from shared online text (as with Kazemi's book), or from programmers sharing so much personal human experience with the machine in the form of passages to pull from, that that enterprise feels anything but creative in an honest way. We would rather just sit down together with pen and paper and use the findings of our research to attempt to write a novel ourselves.

POSTSCRIPT, OR,
SOME BACKGROUND
ON METHOD

A few caveats. This Postscript is designed as a simple bridge—not the Rialto Bridge or the Ponte Vecchio—but a *simple* bridge, like a long plank crossing a ravine, from the world of fictional stories into the terrain of text mining. What follows is not designed for the computer scientist, for the professor, or for the engineer in a publishing start-up. It is not going to give you the code you need for sentiment analysis of novels and neither is it going to give you a step-by-step guide in how to make your own bestseller-ometer at home. For those people who are interested in coding, there are many appropriate textbooks and scholarly papers out there that will teach you basic and more advanced approaches to the computational analysis of text. Similarly, these closing pages are not specifically aimed at the big lover of fiction or the budding novelist either. There will be a few examples of computer outputs and basic talk of things like "parsing," "machine learning,"

and "Named Entity Recognition." Our aim here is simply to offer a rudimentary introduction to some of the methods behind
the findings in this book.

There are two broad key terms in the method we used
for classifying books, and they constitute two overarching
steps in the process. These terms—"text mining" and "machine
learning"—are frequently used interchangeably, and in many
ways the processes that each entails are interdependent. Text
mining sometimes uses machine learning, and machine learning requires mined features as input. For our purposes here,
we'll separate the two. Text mining can be defined rather narrowly as the process by which we discover and extract textual
features from a book. It is, therefore, "step one." Machine learning can be defined, also narrowly but sufficiently, as the way in
which we process those features in order to make predictions
about whether a book belongs in the bestselling group or not.
That's "step two." Perfecting each of these steps satisfactorily
enough to present *The Circle* as the paradigmatic example of a
manuscript likely to best sell took us about four years and several thousand computers.

Text Mining

The ways that computers are taught to read are manyfold,
and the details of how all this machine reading gets done is
the subject of an entire field of academic research called
Natural Language Processing (NLP). Scholars working in
this field have developed powerful programs for mining information from the written word. The most basic tasks in NLP are

word segmentation, sentence identification, part of speech tagging, and dependency parsing. They all have their challenges, so "basic" here certainly does not mean "easy." All of these tasks underlie the work of *The Bestseller Code* at the core level.

Word segmentation, simply put, is about teaching computers to recognize where a single word begins and ends. You'd think this was as easy as identifying spaces between words, and often it is. But "often" is not good enough in text mining: there are always those difficult edge cases to address. Consider the last sentence. After the word "mining," there was a colon. That colon after "mining" is not part of the word, so we can't just train our computers to separate words based on where the spaces occur. The machines have to know that "mining" is the word and the colon is a mark of punctuation. Now consider a word such as "doesn't." Is this contracted form of "does not" one word or two? If it is one word, then in this instance the computer must recognize the apostrophe not as a mark of punctuation in the same way as the previous example, but as a stand-in letter. What about "can't" or the possessive "Robert's"? These and other quirks of word usage can be tricky for computers to disambiguate—sometimes they are tricky for human beings. When we ask our students if "can't" is one word or two, about half of them say "one word" and the other half say "two" because they know that "can't" stands for "can not." Then there are those compound words that are sometimes written as two words, sometimes one, and sometimes as two with a hyphen. We had about five discussions while writing this book about one such word: bestseller. Is it best-seller? Do books best sell? Or best-sell? In this respect, contractions and compounds are a bit like Schrödinger's cat: existing in two different states at the same time.

So even a task as apparently simple as word segmentation can be quite complicated once we really dig into the way that language and grammar work. Researchers in NLP have handled these issues by writing programs that reliably segment the words in a document and then offer specific options for how to handle things like contractions and capitalization. In our research on contemporary bestsellers, we had to make many decisions about how to handle precisely these kinds of options, and for different types of tasks we ultimately made different decisions about how we would define a word. When it came to analyzing style, for example, as we did in chapter 4, one decision we made was to ignore uppercase letters and therefore the potential difference between "The" and "the." These were treated as two instances of the same word. But we could have gone the other route, asking the machine to read them differently, and it's possible that we might have learned something very useful from capitalized instances of "the." Consider that a capitalized instance of "The" in a novel is almost always going to appear as the first word of a sentence. In chapter 5, we saw how powerful the word "the" can be in the titles of novels, but what if bestselling authors write more sentences that begin with the word "the"? By choosing to treat all the words as lowercase, we may have missed out on finding a pattern in bestselling style.

Finding where sentences begin and end is another tricky problem for computers. The end of a sentence is typically marked by a period, question mark, or an exclamation point. The beginning of a new sentence is marked by the use of a capital letter. Most of the time, our computers can find the boundary between sentences by looking for these clues. We could write a computer program with a simple rule that says something like this:

> Begin at the first word and scan through the text until encountering a period, a question mark, or an exclamation point. If the next word after the period, question mark, or exclamation point is capitalized, this is a sentence boundary.

But what happens when your program encounters a sentence like this: "I was surprised to hear that Dr. Archer was writing a novel." In this sentence there is a period (after "Dr") followed by the capital letter "A" (in "Archer"). The rule we just gave the computer would, in this case, incorrectly mark a boundary between what it perceives as two sentences. Because of this and other similar issues associated with abbreviations, we cannot simply teach our computer to read sentences based on a rule about end punctuation and capital letters. We need to add additional rules to deal with abbreviations. There are other complicating factors as well. Consider a passage that contains quoted speech such as this:

> After a long day spent training the machine to read bestsellers, Matt called Jodie and said, "Dialog will be the death of me." Jodie offered solace in the form of Scotch whisky.

In this case, the period marking the end of the sentence is found inside a quotation mark. To deal with this situation, our computer needs to be given *another* special rule for handling quotation marks, and it turns out that this exception generally only applies to prose written using American and Canadian conventions. In British and Australian English, the quote marks are typically placed *inside* the punctuation. Given the malleable nature of language, it is not hard to imagine many possible exceptions to these general rules. By now, you get the idea. Even the very basic extraction of features from text is complicated.

For this reason, a lot of work in natural language processing, and text mining more generally, has moved away from rule-based "parsing" (the technical term for breaking sentences apart into units) in favor of methods based on statistical inference. Instead of trying to imagine all the possible ways that language can be written, and then coding a huge set of rules full of exceptions for handling all these different cases, the statistical approach tries to learn the latent rules governing language, by having the machine study and learn the probabilities of different constructions and combinations from real-world examples.

Automated part of speech tagging provides a good example of how this process works. In chapter 2, we wrote about how we studied the nouns in a book in order to learn what its topics were. Before we could apply our topic-modeling algorithms, we first had to have our computer figure out which words were the nouns. The word "hope," for example, might be a noun: "He held out *hope* that she would buy the book her-self." Or it may be a verb: "She *hoped* he would buy her the book." Or it may be a proper noun, such as a person's name: "*Hope* told him to buy the book himself." Modern part of speech taggers have the task of tagging which words in a sentence are verbs, which are nouns, and so on, and they are trained to dis-ambiguate these different meanings. They look at the context of the entire sentence and then infer the most likely part of speech for each word based on position and context.

When we employ a part of speech tagger to these three sen-tences we get an output that looks like this:*

He/PRP held/VBD out/RP hope/NN that/IN she/PRP would/MD buy/VB the/DT book/NN herself/PRP ./.

She/PRP hoped/VBD he/PRP would/MD buy/VB her/PRP the/DT book/NN ./.

Hope/NNP told/VBD him/PRP to/TO buy/VB the/DT book/NN himself/PRP ./.

The capital letters after the slashes are abbreviations for the parts of speech. In the first sentence "hope" is correctly identi-fied as a noun (NN), in the second sentence as a verb (VBD) and in the third as a proper noun (NNP). Once a text is tagged in

---

* If you want to try this out for yourself, the natural language processing group at Stanford University has an online demo at http://nlp.stanford.edu:8080 /parser/index.jsp

this manner, it is easy to write another program that extracts only those words that have been assigned an NN tag. We then have the nouns, which are the basic building blocks in how we start to train the computer to read for topic.

There are a number of ways that researchers have trained programs to infer parts of speech, but most of them start with a big collection of sentences that have been annotated by human beings. Grammar gurus spend many hours identifying the true parts of speech, and then these guru-coded examples are given to the machine as "training data." From this training data, the machine builds a statistical model that can calculate the probability of various combinations of words. For example, the machine might discover that 55 percent of the time the word "the" is followed by a noun and 40 percent of the time by an adjective and 5 percent of the time by a number. As you might imagine, these taggers are not perfect, but they are very close, so close in fact that some researchers consider the computational tagging of parts of speech a "solved problem." That is open to some debate, but not too much. The Stanford Part of Speech Tagger clocks in at between 97 and 100 percent accuracy, and that is certainly good enough for most text-processing tasks, including those we performed in this study of bestsellers.

Named entity recognition (NER) is another closely related type of language processing that we relied on during our research. A named entity, in this case, is a person, place, or organization: Lisbeth Salander, New York City, or Microsoft. This kind of entity recognition enables us to ask questions, for instance, about whether or not the geopolitical setting of a novel significantly influences its likeliness to hit the lists. We did ask this question, of course, and found that while it does matter whether an author chooses a city or the wilderness, the specific city does not matter all that much when it comes to bestselling. A novel set in New York has just as much chance as one set in Stockholm.

In chapter 5 we used NER to help us understand character and the kinds of agency associated with male and female characters. But even more important to our study of character was a technique called dependency parsing. Dependency parsers are programs designed to analyze and map the grammatical structure of sentences. The parser figures out which words go together into phrases and which words constitute the subject, the object, and the verb in a sentence. Like the part of speech taggers described above, a dependency parser uses information from sentences that have been parsed by human beings in order to infer the likely structure of the sentences it is then asked to read. For chapter 5, we wanted to study character agency by exploring the kinds of verbs that are typically found associated with male and female characters.* Consider this sentence from *The Circle*: "Mae knew Renata was watching her, and she knew her face was betraying something like horror." When we run this sentence through a dependency parser, we get the following output:†

---

* The idea of using a dependency parser for this task was originally suggested by two of Matt's graduate students, Gabi Kirilloff and Jonathan Cheng.

† This sentence was parsed using the online demo version of the Stanford Dependency Parser, which you can try out for yourself at http://nlp.stanford .edu:8080/parser/index.jsp

nsubj(knew-2, Mae-1)

root(ROOT-0, knew-2)

nsubj(watching-5, Renata-3)

aux(watching-5, was-4)

ccomp(knew-2, watching-5)

dobj(watching-5, her-6)

cc(knew-2, and-8)

nsubj(knew-10, she-9)

conj(knew-2, knew-10)

nmod:poss(face-12, her-11)

nsubj(betraying-14, face-12)

aux(betraying-14, was-13)

ccomp(knew-10, betraying-14)

dobj(betraying-14, something-15)

case(horror-17, like-16)

nmod(betraying-14, horror-17)

The first line of this output shows the association of the subject "Mae" with the main verb "knew." Incidentally, the numbers next to each word reference the position of the words in the sentence: "Mae" is the first word, then "knew," then "Renata," and so on. Notice too that the parser has also identified the relationship between Renata, another character, and the verb phrase "was watching" and has also identified the pronoun "she" with the other instance of the verb "knew." Combining output from the dependency parser with data about the names of characters found using NER algorithms enabled us to study how different verbs get associated with different types of characters. In this sentence, for example, we observe that the character Mae "knows" and the character Renata "watches."

Dependency parsing was the most computationally intensive natural language processing task we performed in our research. A single novel could take up to fifteen hours to run, and we had thousands of them. And even after the books were parsed in this manner, we still had to process them again in order to extract the particular subject-verb relationships of interest. This is such a laborious process that we relied on a cluster of one thousand computers that could process one thousand books at a time.

From a computational perspective, the work we did to map plotlines using emotional language in chapter 3 was perhaps the simplest. Researchers who work in an area of natural language processing called "sentiment analysis" have developed several different approaches to the study of emotional language. The most sophisticated of these methods use some of the same types of statistical inference techniques used in dependency parsing and part of speech tagging. These methods are currently used to analyze all sorts of customer reviews and to infer sentiment in all sorts of documents including e-mail. We experimented with these more sophisticated techniques, but when it came to identifying the emotionally laden words in fiction, we found that the simpler methods actually outperformed the more complex ones.

The approach we found most effective involved using several special dictionaries of emotional words. These dictionaries, called sentiment lexicons, are basically just lists of words that have been given either a positive or negative polarity or valence. "Love," for example, is marked as a very positive emotional word, and it follows that "hate" is a very negative one. We trained our model to read through a novel one word at a time, note whether each word was in one of the sentiment lexicons, and then score the sentences. Patterns of positive and negative sentences in emotional terms create the curves of the plotlines in chapter 3. Consider this sentence spoken by Eamon in *The Circle*: "I love you as the grass loves the dew, as the birds love a bough." That's the kind of sentiment that the algorithm will give a positive score. Here is another line from *The Circle*, this time from the scene in which Annie has just learned that her ancestors were slave owners: "I mean, do you know the chaos this is wreaking on my family?" Unsurprisingly, this is a sentence the algorithm labeled as belonging in negative terrain. The frequency of these positive or negative sentences in a given passage tends to show us something about the fate of our protagonist and where we are in a plot.

All of the text mining processes discussed so far are about detecting and extracting features. Once words are segmented, it is easy to count how often they occur. Once sentence boundaries are identified, we can calculate such things as average sentence length and the ratio of sentences in dialog to sentences of pure narration. After we have performed part of speech tagging, we can explore the types of nouns and verbs and adjectives that different authors use, and we can even begin to look for patterns that are typical to certain writers and not others. We can use the nouns we've extracted as input to our topic-modeling algorithms (as we did in chapter 2), and the dependency-parsed data allows us to examine the syntax of sentences and to look at the kind of relationships that authors establish between subjects and verbs.

All of this computational work is really the preparation stage. It is typically summarized as a "pre-" process of feature identification and extraction. It is only after we have explored every possible means of extracting features of interest that we can do the more exciting work of using them to classify books. This second phase of building the bestseller-ometer is called machine learning.

Machine Learning

Machine learning is all about sifting the features mined during the text mining stage. During the early research stage for this book, we parsed 28,000 features. With machine learning and classification experiments, the goal is to determine which of these have predictive value. In this long process, we eliminated thousands of features. Ultimately, we got to a core set of 2,799 that we believe are genuinely predictive. So we threw out "New York" and "Stockholm," and we threw out numbers like "1984" and "1,000,000", but we noted the usefulness of the topic Human Closeness (chapter 2), of the verbs "need" and "want" (chapter 5), and the contractions "I'm" and "couldn't" (chapter 4). These significant features were brought to our attention thanks to machine-learning algorithms.

The basic idea behind the classification we did in our bestseller research is simple. We start training from the stance that the book world is black and white and that there are only two types (or classes) of books. There are those that hit the bestseller list and those that do not.* We then take all the features mined from those books in our collection that hit the *NYT* list and all the features mined from those books in our collection that did not sell well. The first task is simply to compare them and look for significant differences. If there are big differences in the way that a certain feature is used—perhaps the word "and" is twice as common in bestsellers, or the words "very" and "passion" are used far less—then we can consider that feature useful. Single words like this are obviously very simple examples that may not mean all that much to readers, but once we aggregate single words and uses of grammar into topics and plotlines, then we have powerful, meaningful data.

For this research, we deployed three different types of machine classifiers. All of these algorithms begin by "mapping" every book into what is called a feature space. The number of dimensions in this space is equal to the number of features we want to study. In other words, it's massive. Since it is pretty hard for human beings to mentally conceptualize multidimensional spaces, we'll pretend for the sake of illustration that there are

---

* Obviously the real world is more complex, and if we had had actual sales data, we might have used that instead of the binary value of whether or not a book hit the *NYT* list. Had we had that kind of data, we also would have employed an entirely different set of prediction algorithms. It's worth noting that during our first experiments we took three classes—number ones, novels that charted but did not make the top spot, and non-bestsellers. Amazingly, the models were able to determine the difference between a number-one bestseller and a novel that hit numbers 2-15 on the *NYT* list 80 percent of the time. The same was true of double-digit books—those that stay on the lists for months. Those kinds of nuances were too nuanced for the story of this book, but they were fascinating to observe.

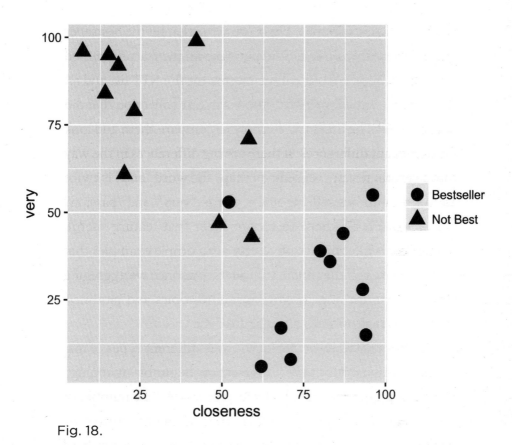

Fig. 18.

only two features in our bestseller-ometer. Let's take two of
the actual 2,799 that matter: the topic Human Closeness and the
single word "very." For every book, the model gives us one
measurement telling us how much Human Closeness there is
and a second measurement telling us how frequently the word
"very" appears. Using these two measurements, we can plot
every one of our books on a two-dimensional grid that might
look something like Figure 18. Each mark on the graph is a
single novel mapped by just those two features.

When you study this graph you will notice that, in general, bestsellers tend to cluster in the lower right corner. The graph tells us they have more human closeness (along the x axis) and use less of the word "very" (the y-axis). If you have read this whole book carefully, you'll already know this from the chapters on topic and style. You might even remember that "really" is a more favorable word than "very" in bestsellers, which we think tells us something about contemporary register and voice. It won't be a surprise to you, then, to see those triangles in the top left corner: these stories are "very" this, and "very" that, and "very" the other, but they are not very successful in realizing compelling human relationships on the page.

The first classification method we used is known as K Nearest Neighbors (KNN). KNN starts by mapping the data just as we have done in this plot. "K" refers to the size of a neighborhood, or an area on the graph. As researchers, we then define what we think is a sensible value for K. So let's say that we set K to equal five. The KNN algorithm starts with one book and then looks at the five other books that are closest to it on the grid (i.e. within the "neighborhood" of five). If the majority of those five books are bestsellers, then the machine will guess that the novel being examined is also a bestseller because the books in that neighborhood have common features that often hit the lists. It's a birds-of-a-feather-flock-together kind of algorithm, and when we are looking at thousands of features and not just the two that were used to make these plots, there are a lot of feathers. Notice in the graph that there is one bestseller closer to the cluster of non-bestsellers in the upper left.

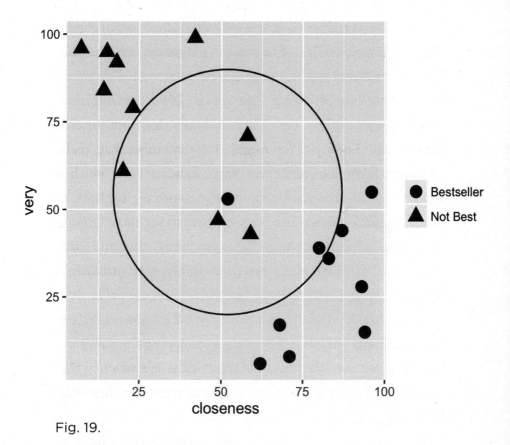

Fig. 19.

In this case, the KNN algorithm is going to look at the five closest books and guess incorrectly that the book is a non-bestseller. It will do this because four out of the five closest books are not bestsellers. The neighborhood is shown circled in figure 19.

All of the other bestsellers in this fake example will be properly classified based on the five books in their immediate neighborhood. The single non-bestseller that is closest to the lower right corner will likely be misclassified as a bestseller since the five books nearest to it include three bestsellers and only two non-bestsellers. These kind of mistakes help explain why our accuracy was an average of 80 percent.

The other two algorithms that we employed are a bit more complicated than KNN. One is called Support Vector Machines (or SVM) and the other is an algorithm called Nearest Shrunken Centroids (NSC). The latter was originally developed for classifying types of cancer based on gene expression data and has been repurposed for research such as ours. Like KNN, SVM and NSC also both work by mapping every book into a multi-dimensional feature space. After this mapping, the SVM algorithm tries to find a maximally sized gap between the known bestsellers and the known non-bestsellers. This gap, or boundary might look something like figure 20.[*]

When an unknown book is mapped into this space, it is then classified as being a bestseller or not based on which side of the gap it falls onto.

The NSC algorithm shares some conceptual similarities with both KNN and SVM. It begins by mapping all the books into the space, and it then identifies the mathematical center point of all the books that are bestsellers and the mathematical center point of all the books that are not bestsellers. It then uses a threshold parameter to shrink these "centroids." An unknown manuscript is classified according to which of the shrunken centroids it maps nearest to.[†]

---

[*] To make the gap easier to see, we've changed the mapping of the books in order to remove the ones on the border.

[†] The details of the learning algorithms we used involve some rather complex mathematics. There is an excellent overview of both KNN and SVM in *An Intro-*

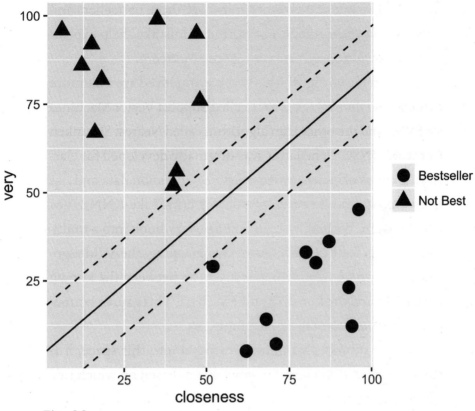

Fig. 20.

Using 2,799 features, the best of our three models (KNN) was able to differentiate between bestsellers and non-bestsellers 90 percent of the time.[*] The worst of our models (SVM) only

---

duction to Statistical Learning by James, Witten, Hastie, and Tibshirani. Springer: New York, 2013. A very brief description of Nearest Shrunken Centroids can be found online at http://statweb.stanford.edu/~tibs/PAM/Rdist/howwork.html along with a link to the academic paper "Diagnosis of multiple cancer types by shrunken centroids of gene expression," in which the algorithm was first tested. Interested readers might also wish to consult: Jockers, Matthew L. and Daniela M. Witten. "A Comparative Study of Machine Learning Methods for Authorship Attribution." *Literary and Linguistic Computing*, 25.2, 2010, 215-224.

[*] We experimented with different values for K and got the best results with K=15.

managed to guess the class correctly 70 percent of the time. NSC was near the middle at 79 percent, but NSC had a distinct advantage over KNN when it came to interpretability. NSC provides a lot of useful data about which features were most helpful to the machine in distinguishing between classes. Overall the average of the three methods was 80 percent, and we used all three to create an "ensemble" prediction for each and every manuscript in our corpus.

At this point, you may be wondering how we derived these percentages. We begin with a collection of bestselling and non-bestselling books. With these two training sets of books—bestsellers and non-bestsellers, we were able to study our model's performance. We did that by first training a model using a randomly selected subset of the total books. The computer used this sample to learn which features differentiated the bestsellers and non-bestsellers in that random set. Using this information, we asked it to classify all the books we had kept out of the learning stage. The machine then made a guess about each of those books, either that they did or did not hit the lists. Note that the machine has no data other than the unmarked manuscripts at this stage. We then check its guesses against what historically happened. This process, called "cross-validation" is what gave us confidence in the project. We used two approaches. For the first, called "10-fold cross-validation," the computer randomly selected 10 percent of the bestsellers and 10 percent of the non-bestsellers to hold out. A model was then trained using the remaining books and then tested by classifying the held-out books. This process of random selection and model building is repeated over and over again

and the classification accuracy is recorded after each validation. We then calculated the average accuracy across all the
repetitions.*

The second cross-validation method is called "hold one out"
validation, and as its name suggests, it involves holding out just
one book at a time. In this process, we took one book out of
the collection and built a model from all of the remaining
books. We then sent the held-out book to the trained model for
a prediction. The prediction was recorded. Then the next book
was held out and the model rebuilt from all of the remaining
data, and this process was repeated over and over again until
every book had been held out and classified.† It is a thorough
and fairly complicated process, and in truth, our model building and testing was quite a bit more rigorous than this brief
overview might suggest. Since there are many more non-
bestselling books in our library, we conducted two types of
experiments, some of which "balanced" the number of books
used in the training so that there were an equal number of
training books from each class. In the balanced experiments,
the model randomly selects a subset of non-bestsellers from
the total number of non-bestsellers available. In this way the
number of bestsellers and non-bestsellers used in training is

---

* We also study the resulting confusion matrices, in order to better understand
our model's precision and recall, but that is a bit beyond the scope of this postscript.

† For a more detailed but still not-too-technical description of text mining and
machine learning, see Jockers, Matthew L. and Underwood, Ted, "Text-Mining
the Humanities." In *New Companion to the Digital Humanities*. Eds. Susan Sch-
reibman, Ray Siemens, and John Unsworth. Wiley-Blackwell.

the same. This class balancing insures that the prior probability of selecting one class over the other is 50/50.

In addition to conducting a series of experiments in which we controlled for class size, we also implemented a procedure of "author control" that insured that we were not giving the very prolific authors an undue advantage. When we ran our hold one out testing, we configured the experiment so that there were no books by the author of the held-out book available in the training data. Had we not done this, the franchise writers such as Grisham, Patterson, and Steel would have had an unfair advantage. They entered this research with the same chance as every other writer.

When we first started our training, several years ago, we tested the viability of Jodie's hypothesis that bestsellers have latent DNA by working with thousands of books that were published before 2010. We wanted a model that gave us good classification performance, eliminated flukes, and offered data that would make human sense to book experts. We were impressed with the results from this first model, and we then watched the book market for a few years. The first model was first trained, for example, without *Fifty Shades of Grey* and without *Gone Girl*. We had to know if it would correctly classify those new books that entered the market. Of course, if you have read chapters 3 and 5 you'll know it did, and that we have learned more about plot and character from those classifications. We keep learning and update the model and retrain when an E. L. James or a new Pulitzer writer comes along, but at this stage it might be true to say that the learning is really for our own human interest rather than to improve the algorithms. Over the past few years, we have been very anxious to absorb new trends into the model—new fads, changes in direction of literary style, and so on. Of course, there's a responsibility to research that makes us do that. But what at first startled us, and now delights us, is that the machine keeps it cool when we feed it the so-called "big new thing." We thought our machine might fail in classifying a book like *Fifty Shades* with all its sex, or a book like *Dragon Tattoo* with its totally new kind of heroine. But it didn't.

The correct classifications of "flukes" in the market like *Fifty Shades* or another very different self-published novel, the Christian novel *The Shack*, have made us think about whether any of these stories are really all that new. If anything, this research has made us stop worrying about fads and zeitgeists and has added weight to the old adage that there are only a handful of stories that just get reinvented and retold, albeit sometimes in a more effective rendition. So the market may have been surprised and will continue to be surprised—foiled by red herrings of "newness"—but on the whole the model has not been. The new topic or character that captures press attention is often just a small part of a novel's DNA as a whole. The model's correct classification of *Fifty Shades* showed, for example, that if BDSM was new to the lists with E. L. James, then just about every other aspect of her novel was not. It taught us that riding crops and blindfolds are just the icing, or perhaps the distraction, in the hands of an author who can weave the more latent aspects of bestselling, right down to comma and verb use, into huge success. The same is true of Lee Child, of Nicholas Sparks, of Dave Eggers, of Toni Morrison, and in fact of all the authors in the computer's recommended reading list.

We hope you enjoy them as we have.